MODERN

DEFENSIVE
FOOTBALL

MODERN
DEFENSIVE
FOOTBALL

GOMER JONES
*Line Coach, The University
of Oklahoma*

CHARLES (BUD) WILKINSON
Football Coach, The University of Oklahoma

PRENTICE-HALL, INC.
Englewood Cliffs, N. J.

L. C. Cat. Card No.: 57-10410

Fifth printing.......*February, 1961*

Printed in U.S.A.
59110—C

Contents

Foreword, by Tim Cohane . . . . .   *ix*

Preface . . . .   *xi*

1. Introduction *1*

2. Objectives of Defense *7*

3. Basic Theory of Team Defense . .   *12*

4. Individual Defensive Fundamentals *22*

   FUNDAMENTALS FOR LINEMEN, *29*

   DRILLS TO TEACH FUNDAMENTAL DEFENSIVE LINE PLAY, *36*

   FUNDAMENTALS FOR LINEBACKERS, *42*

   FUNDAMENTALS FOR THE PLAY OF DEFENSIVE ENDS, *47*

   FUNDAMENTALS FOR SECONDARY MEN, *48*

   SUMMARY, *51*

Contents

5. **The Two Distinct Units of the Defensive Team** 52

6. **Play of the Containing Portion of the Defensive Team** 58

PLAY OF THE FOUR-SPOKE CONTAIN-ING UNIT, *61*

ASSIGNMENTS FOR THE CORNER MEN, *61*

ASSIGNMENTS FOR DEEP SAFETIES, *66*

ADJUSTMENTS TO FLANKERS — DEEP SAFETIES, *69*

PLAY OF THE FIVE-SPOKE CONTAIN-ING UNIT, *72*

PLAY OF THE ENDS—FIVE-SPOKE DE-FENSE, *73*

PLAY OF THE WIDE SAFETY MEN—FIVE-SPOKE DEFENSE, *76*

PLAY OF THE MIDDLE SAFETY MAN—FIVE-SPOKE DEFENSE, *79*

ADJUSTMENTS TO FLANKERS—FIVE-SPOKE DEFENSE, *80*

7. **Play of the Forcing Unit of the Defense** 85

8. **Proper Utilization of Personnel** 89

9. **Defense 72** 93

10. **Defense 54** 107

11. **Defense 45** 114

12. Defense 60 .... **124**

ASSIGNMENTS FOR "60 INSIDE," *126*
60 OUTSIDE, *128*
REGULAR 60, *129*
60 INSIDE AND 60 OUTSIDE, *130*
CROSS CHARGE 60, *131*
TIGHT TACKLE 60, *134*

13. Defense 53 .... **137**

14. Defense 70 .... **151**

70 INSIDE, *153*
70 OUTSIDE, *155*

15. Goal Line Defenses **159**

ADJUSTMENTS TO FLANKERS IN "8-3"
GOAL LINE DEFENSES, *166*
SEVEN-FOUR GOAL LINE DEFENSE, *168*
ADJUSTMENTS TO FLANKERS IN
SEVEN-FOUR GOAL LINE DEFENSE, *170*

16. Defense vs. Single-Wing **172**

DEFENSE 72 VS. SINGLE-WING, *175*
STUNTS FROM DEFENSE 72, *184*
DEFENSE 72 LEFT, *185*
DEFENSE 72 RIGHT, *188*
DEFENSE 60 VS. SINGLE-WING, *192*
DEFENSE 60 LEFT, *195*
DEFENSE 60 RIGHT, *197*
TACKLE CROSS CHARGE, *198*
SUMMARY, *199*

Contents

17. **Spread Defense** *202*

18. **Pass Defense** *210*

PLAY OF THE FOUR-SPOKE CONTAIN-
ING UNIT ON PASS DEFENSE, *233*

PLAY OF THE MIDDLE OR DEEP SAFE-
TIES ON THE FOUR-SPOKE PASS DE-
FENSE, *237*

PLAY OF THE FIVE-SPOKE CONTAIN-
ING UNIT ON PASS DEFENSE, *242*

PLAY OF THE OUTSIDE SAFETY MEN,
244

PLAY OF THE MIDDLE SAFETY MAN,
247

19. **Defensive Strategy** *249*

20. **Conclusion** *258*

Index *267*

Foreword

This book treats
of the most important thing in football—defense.
Specifically, it discusses individual fundamentals
and team patterns of present-day defense.

In roughly the last two decades, the field tactics
of the great American college game have experi-
enced two far-reaching and basic developments.
One is the varying movements of the defense both
before and at the snapback of the ball. The other is
the delayed commitment of the offense after the ball
is snapped, until the defense has *definitely com-
mitted itself.*

Both developments have received lasting contri-
butions from the work of Charles Burnham (Bud)
Wilkinson, his co-worker Gomer Jones, and the rest
of the coaching staff at the University of Oklahoma.

The impressive succession of national and Big
Seven Conference championships won by Oklahoma

—at this writing the current winning streak of the Sooners has reached an all-time modern record of 40—has proven the value of thoroughly thought-out and precisely executed defenses. These defenses are even more important to the astonishing saga of accomplishment than the more eye-catching machinations of the split or shuttle-T formation. Their story and their execution by individual and team are all set down in this book.

Not only Oklahoma, but college football in general, owes much to Wilkinson and his staff. They rate high, if not at the very top, of those modern staffs which have proved it is not only possible, but entirely salutary, to turn out championship teams year after year by skillfully organizing and training personnel of high caliber as students as well as athletes.

And now, in the category of clinical football, Bud and Gomer (who, as the Sooner State couplet has it, "Go together like Greek and Homer") have provided a guide of inestimable value to coaches and all students of the game at the post-graduate, college, and high school levels. I guarantee that anybody who picks it up will not want to put it down before the last whistle.

TIM COHANE

Preface

It is the authors'
purpose in the Preface to state briefly the plan of
the book.

At the outset, we would like to admit frankly that,
to our knowledge, there is no truly perfect plan of
defensive football. The rules of the game are reasonably well balanced between the offense and defense.
However, the rules do give a slight advantage to
the offense. If the offensive team is well-coached
and well-conditioned and if its personnel is physically equal to that of the defensive team, the offense
should be able to move the ball with reasonable
consistency. Therefore, we do not know of, nor believe there is, any defense which will completely
stop the opponent. In this sense of "stopping the
opponent," we mean holding them to absolutely no
gain for several successive plays.

We feel it is realistic to assume that the offensive

team will move the ball reasonably well. Thus, the mission of the defense becomes one of "slowing up" the opponents, of keeping them from making the long gain or the easy touchdown, and of battling them to gain possession of the ball before they can score.

This book, then, is not intended to create the idea that there is any defense that will completely and totally control the offensive team. Rather, we hope to present a theory of defensive play that we feel, to a degree, will contain the offensive opponent.

The book is divided into four major categories. These are:

1. Basic theory of defensive football.
2. Basic fundamentals of defensive play.
3. Individual defensive assignments within the team pattern.
4. Defensive strategy.

The authors acknowledge their indebtedness to many people. First, to the other members of the coaching staff of the University of Oklahoma, who, during recent years, through their excellent instruction on the field, have made this theory of defense succeed in actual game competition.

We are also grateful for the fine instruction we received as players and assistant coaches. Bernie Bierman and Dr. George Hauser of the University of Minnesota, Francis Schmidt of Ohio State, Ossie Solem of the University of Iowa, Syracuse, and Springfield College, together with Lowell "Red" Dawson of Tulane and Pittsburgh, are responsible for our background in the game. Further, we would like to acknowledge the great debt we owe those coaches whose original ideas are the basis of our theory of defensive football. The foremost of these men, without doubt, is General Bob Neyland, the great coach of the University of Tennessee. In essence, the theory of defense which will be presented in this book is an adaptation of the patterns developed by the great defensive master, General Neyland. In addition, we have had the good fortune to spend a great many hours with Bobby Dodd and Ray Graves of Georgia Tech. In our opinion, these men have been the leaders in the development of defensive football among modern coaches.

Last but not least, we would like to pay our respects and acknowledge our debt to the great players of the University of Oklahoma. These men, in recent years, by their untiring effort and unselfish devotion, have made these theories of defense hold up in actual play.

1

Introduction

In any discussion of football, it is of paramount importance always to remember that the theoretical ideas of the coach must be executed by individual, human young men. The success of any theory depends on the physical ability and mental attitude of the player. The ability and attitude of the individual player become and remain the most important factors in the ultimate success of the team.

There is a great deal of discussion among coaches and fans as to the relative values of pure physical ability as compared to mental toughness. In the opinion of the authors, mental toughness—the willingness to pay a price in practice for victory—is a far more important attribute for a football player than physical ability. If two players have the psychological quality of mental toughness in equal amount, the boy with superior physical prowess will, of course, win. However, physical ability alone will never defeat superior mental attitude. Mental attitude creates within the player the will to win, the desire, through proper conditioning, to develop his physical ability to the fullest possible extent.

From the individual's standpoint, the game of football comprises three basic fundamentals. These are: (1) blocking, (2) tackling, and (3) moving. Each man must master these three fundamentals if he is to become a capable player. The first two, blocking and tackling, are obvious. If the player has the ability to block, he can play sound, fundamental, offensive football. Given the ability to tackle, he can play good defensive football. But both of these abilities are based on the third, and by far the most important, fundamental, that of the ability to move.

The vital importance of the ability to move or run is often overlooked by football fans and coaches. The game itself is one hundred per cent a game of movement. At the start of each play both teams are lined up waiting for the center to snap the ball. As the ball is snapped, all twenty-two men on both teams must move. The fundamentals of blocking and tackling can never be used unless a boy possesses the ability to move quickly and accurately. The player must first move into position to block before he can execute the fundamental of blocking. Similarly, he must move to the ball carrier before he can make the tackle.

There are certain secondary fundamentals which make up the game. None of these fundamentals need to be executed by every man on the team. However, somewhere among the eleven men who comprise the team there must be individuals who can place-kick, punt, throw the ball, catch it, and execute the other minor techniques of the game. In the opinion of the authors, these minor fundamentals are seldom worth the practice time that is spent on them. Superior execution of the basic fundamentals mentioned above usually will insure victory. The main emphasis of the coaching staff should be placed on the proper development of blocking, tackling, and running.

The game of football, from a theoretical standpoint, is divided into three major phases. There are: (1) offense, (2) defense, and (3) the kicking game. This book is concerned with the second of these three basic phases, that of defense.

Without question, defense is the most important single phase of the game. This blunt statement, I know, will be doubted by many students of football who may feel that offense is more important. Some others, perhaps, believe that the kicking game, properly developed, can pay bigger dividends toward

3

victory than can defensive football. Since the authors feel unequivocally that defense far, far transcends in importance the other two phases of the game, it would perhaps be well to clarify and substantiate this statement.

In analyzing the importance of defensive football, it is obvious that, *if the defense is strong enough the opponent will never score.* It follows logically that if the opponent does not score, your team cannot be defeated.

In pursuing this theory further, if the opponent can be held scoreless, it is possible for your team to score one almost lucky touchdown and thereby gain a victory. This happened in the Orange Bowl game, January 1, 1954, when Oklahoma defeated the University of Maryland. During the game, Maryland played very sound offensive and defensive football. At no time did Oklahoma threaten to score except during the second quarter when they made one reasonably sustained drive, climaxed by the perfect execution of an end run to score a touchdown. The Oklahoma offense in no way dominated the Maryland defense, but since Maryland was held scoreless, Oklahoma was able to win the game 7-0.

If the defense is sound, even though the opponent does score, it is virtually impossible for them to score enough points to demoralize your team.

As long as your team remains within striking distance of victory, they will continue to fight hard and to play the full sixty minutes of the game to the limit of their ability. If your defense maintains reasonable control of the game and if your team does not get too far behind, it can rally and win in the final moments of the contest. Only a sound defense can maintain this opportunity throughout a game.

For example, in 1950 the University of Oklahoma was playing the University of Kansas in a game which to all intents and purposes would decide the Big Seven championship. The Kansas team completely dominated the first half and was leading 7-0 at that point. At the start of the third quarter, Kansas again scored and was leading 13-0. Through the first three quarters of the game Kansas had been dominant not only on offense but on defense as well. However, the Oklahoma team, through a reasonably sound execution of defensive football, had stayed within striking distance of victory. At the start of the fourth quarter, Oklahoma was able to rally, score, and to kick the extra point. That left the score 13-7. One more touchdown would insure victory. When the tide begins to run, as often happens, it picks up momentum. Oklahoma was fortunate enough to be able to score again within a short period of time and went on to win the game 33-13. However, it must be remembered that without a sound defense, Oklahoma would have been so far behind at the end of the first three quarters that they could not have rallied to win.

Because of the facts stated above, and the examples given, we believe that defense is the most important single phase of football. This fact is true because:

1. If the opponent does not score, you cannot be defeated.

2. If the opponent is held to a very few points, the defensive team maintains a chance, throughout the game, to win.

3. You must stop the opponent and gain possession of the ball before you can use your own offense.

It therefore follows that in building a football team, sound defense is the most important single objective.

2

Objectives of the
Defense

The major objective of all defensive football is to keep the opponent from scoring. Every member of the defensive team should have this fact uppermost in mind at all times. To repeat, the first and only mission of the defense is *to prevent a score*. Strange at it may seem, defensive players often lose sight of this vital fact.

If the offensive team begins to move the ball reasonably well and if they complete a few short hook passes for a succession of steady gains, some defensive halfbacks forget that their mission is to prevent a touchdown. As the next hook pass begins to develop, the halfback comes up quickly to prevent the completion. As he comes up, the offense, anticipating this movement, fakes the hook and throws deep for the touchdown. The defensive player in this instance has overlooked or momentarily forgotten the major objective of his play, which is, at all times, *to prevent a score*.

The second objective of the defensive team is to gain possession of the ball. This objective is always secondary to the first objective stated above. The defensive team can gain possession of the ball in three ways:

1. Recovering a fumble.
2. Intercepting a pass.
3. Keeping the opposing team from making a first down.

Most defensive players think only in terms of the third item, that of keeping the offensive team from making a first down. Since the offensive team can put the ball in play four times before the defense can gain possession of the ball, defensive players should think in terms of forcing a fumble or intercepting a pass on every play.

By these methods the defense can gain possession of the ball in one play.

The third objective of the defense is to *score while on defense*. General Bob Neyland has aptly pointed out that the defense can score in more ways than the offense. The defense can score in the following manner:

1. By intercepting a pass and returning it for a touchdown.

2. By returning a kick for a touchdown.

3. By blocking a kick and recovering it for a touchdown.

4. By forcing a fumble and catching the ball in the air to score.

Whenever the defense is able to score in one of the manners outlined above, it gains a tremendous psychological advantage over the opponent. The offensive team with the ball in its possession is mentally geared to making a gain and scoring a touchdown. The psychological boomerang and shock of a play, initiated by it, resulting in a touchdown for the opponent, is often so great that the team involved is never again able to rally and move on to victory.

In the Orange Bowl game of 1956, the University of Oklahoma and the University of Maryland were battling on reasonably even terms throughout the first fifty minutes. Oklahoma had a small lead which was gained by a reasonably successful touchdown drive against a very stout Maryland defense. With only ten minutes to play, Maryland was still very much in the game. They had moved the ball from their own 40 yard line to the Oklahoma 26. At that point, Carl Dodd intercepted a Maryland pass and returned it 82 yards for an Oklahoma touchdown. For all intents and purposes, the game was over.

In 1949, the University of Oklahoma and the University of Missouri were playing late in the season for the Big Seven championship. At the end of the first half the score was 7-7. Missouri had made a total of 99 net yards; Oklahoma had gained a total of 97 net yards. The first half was as even as any football game could possibly be.

At the start of the second half, Oklahoma kicked off to Missouri. The Tigers were held for three successive plays. They punted on the fourth down, and Jack Mitchell of Oklahoma returned the punt 65 yards for a touchdown. This so shocked the Missouri team that Oklahoma scored three times in the next four minutes, and eventually won the game 41-7.

The psychological effect of the punt return on the Missouri team changed the game completely. What had been a desperately fought, absolutely even contest resulted in an easy victory.

Against the Oklahoma Aggies in 1952, Oklahoma again found themselves in an even, tough, bitter ball game. With the score tied 7-7, the Aggies were forced to kick. Bo Bolinger, of Oklahoma, broke through and blocked the punt. He recovered the ball and ran 32 yards for an Oklahoma touchdown. Again the psychological shock of this decisive single defensive play so upset the Aggies that they failed to regain their equilibrium and Oklahoma went on to win by a large score.

If the defensive team can become offensive minded, to the degree that they honestly expect to score while on defensive, they will execute every phase of the defensive plan better. However, every member of the defensive team must recognize, *in the proper sequence*, the objectives of his defensive play. To repeat, these are:

1. To prevent a score.
2. To gain possession of the ball.
3. Whenever possible, to score while on defense.

3

Basic Theory of Team Defense

Since the first objective of defense is to prevent a score, it follows that any defensive plan must first be designed to prevent one play, easy touchdowns.

It is impossible defensively to separate the theories of defense against runs and defense against passes. The two must blend into a single whole and be mutually self-supporting. If the defensive team knew before the ball was snapped whether the play would be a run or a pass, the defensive task would be only half as difficult. However, they have no way of ascertaining this fact until after the play begins. Since passing is the truly lethal weapon of the offensive team, the defense should always play for a pass first and then for a run.

The one play, long pass touchdown, is to football what the home run is to baseball. It results in an easy victory for the offensive team. Therefore, all defense football is basically pass defense. If your pass defense is adequate and holds up well enough to contain the offensive team and keep them from throwing the touchdown pass, you have the essential element of a sound defense. If they cannot do this *all of the time*, the defense will never be adequate.

In the Sugar Bowl game of 1951, the University of Oklahoma met the University of Kentucky. The Oklahoma offensive was reasonably successful throughout the game. Oklahoma averaged 6.3 yards per try offensively. Defensively they contained Kentucky quite well. However, in the first series of downs Oklahoma fumbled, giving Kentucky the ball on the Oklahoma 22 yard line. From that point Babe Parilli threw a touchdown pass. Later in the first half Oklahoma again fumbled and Kentucky recovered at mid-field. Again Parilli threw for a breakaway touchdown. Kentucky won the game 13-7 because of the failure of Oklahoma's pass defense to stop the long, one play touchdown pass.

In 1948, when Oklahoma played Santa Clara in Kezar Stadium, the Sooners led at the end of the first quarter 10-0. They had completely dominated the game on both offense and defense. Two minutes before the end of the first half Santa Clara completed a 48 yard touchdown pass. In the third quarter, the Broncos threw two more one play, breakaway touchdown passes. The final score, Santa Clara 21, Oklahoma 17. Santa Clara had hit three "home runs" and the resulting 21 points provided the margin of victory.

In both of these games, Oklahoma had failed to defend adequately in depth. The offensive pass receivers got behind all Oklahoma defenders and scored the easy touchdown.

From the theoretical standpoint, in order to prevent the easy score, the defensive team must *contain the offense.* By containing the offense we mean that the defensive team deploys and moves in such a manner that they always keep the ball inside of, and/or in front of, some member of the defensive team. If this can be done, the one play breakaway touchdown will be prevented.

A considerable portion of the defensive team must be devoted to this "containing" phase of play. If the ball is to be contained laterally on both sides, and kept in front of some defensive player, a reasonable number of men, usually four or five, must maneuver on each play in the proper manner to accomplish the objective.

With four or five men devoted to containing the offense, the remaining six or seven men probably will not be capable of stopping every play at the line of scrimmage, and the defense will be "somewhat soft" for a straight ahead, quick, hard-hitting attack. However, these short gains seldom result in touchdowns.

Mathematically, factors tend to favor the defense if the single play long-gain touchdown is eliminated. Most offensive teams can put the ball in play only eight or ten times without making a mechanical offensive error. After the first eight or ten plays of a sustained sequence have been run, the percentages favoring offensive mistakes become greater and greater with every additional play. Each time the offense puts the ball in play, there is a greater chance of their making a mistake, resulting in the defense gaining possession of the ball.

The most probable errors of the offensive team are as follows:

1. Fumble.

2. Pass interception.

3. Penalty (back field in motion, offside, use of hands, and so forth).

4. Missed assignment (an offensive player blocking the wrong defensive opponent and allowing another defensive player to move in free to the ball carrier).

As has been stated, most offensive teams can avoid

these errors the first few times they put the ball in play. However, with each succeeding down the percentages favoring an error increase almost geometrically. Very few offensive teams are able to put the ball in play between twenty and thirty times without making one of the errors listed above, any one of which probably will result in the defensive team gaining possession of the ball.

Because of this fact (the truth of which may be doubted by some), the defensive team should rely on the *containing portion* of their defense to *delay* the offensive team by holding them to short gains. Ultimately, this delaying tactic will force the defense to put the ball in play numerous times before they can possibly score. Then in all probability, the offense, during the course of their sustained drive, will make a mistake which will enable the defensive team to gain possession of the ball. Perhaps some examples are in order.

In the Sugar Bowl game between Kentucky and Oklahoma in 1951, which has been previously mentioned, Oklahoma never came into possession of the ball except in their own half of the field. Most of the time they were deep in their own territory, that is, behind their own 30 yard line, when they received the ball on a first down and ten. Almost every time the Sooners got the ball, they were able to move it for at least two or three and sometimes four or five first downs. However, the gains were always reasonably short and, except for one series of plays during which the Sooners sustained the ball for an 83 yard touchdown drive, the percentages caught up with them before they could score. After a few plays the fumble or the penalty or the assignment error occurred, the Sooners failed to make the first down, and they were forced to kick. Even though Oklahoma gained 320 yards during the game, they scored only 7 points, which was not enough for victory.

During the Sugar Bowl game of January 1, 1956 between Georgia Tech and Pitt, the same pattern for the game was most apparent. Each time Pitt had the ball they started a smooth offensive drive toward the Georgia Tech goal line. However, only one time during the game were they able to sustain the drive to a touchdown without making an error. Even though the Panthers gained 284 yards, they scored only 7 points and were defeated 13-7.

These two games are perfect examples of the *containing-delaying* theory of defense in actual game competition.

The concept of this theory of defense may be more readily understood if an explanation of the diametrically opposite plan is outlined. The objective of this defensive idea is to hold the opponent to absolutely no gain on each and every play. In order to do this, it is necessary to commit, with the snap of the ball, many members of the defensive team in an attempt to charge hard enough to gain penetration into the offensive backfield. If such tactics are successful, the offense will not gain and a loss will probably result. However, if an offensive back breaks past this concentrated rush on the part of the defensive team, there will be so few defensive men remaining that the play will result in a long gain or a touchdown.

Many teams have a tendency to use this plan, that is, to play what amounts to a goal line defense out on the field of play in all short yardage situations. In the past we have done this at the University of Oklahoma. However, in 1950 in our game against Nebraska the danger of these tactics became so apparent to us that since that time we have always "defended in depth" when the ball is out on the field of play.

In the Nebraska game, Oklahoma was leading 14-0 at the end of the first quarter. Nebraska returned the next kick off almost to the midfield strip. Here they came into a third down, 2 yards to gain situation. Oklahoma went into a goal line defense. The ball was snapped, and Bobby Reynolds broke through the middle and went 52 yards to score. Nebraska kicked off to Oklahoma, the Sooners fum-

Illustration No. 1. Tackling: pre-contact.

Illustration No. 2. Tackling: moment of contact (head on ball).

Illustration No. 3. Tackling: lift from ground.

Illustration No. 4. Tackling: finish.

bled on first down, and Nebraska came into possession on the Oklahoma 28. They ran three plays, netting 9 yards. It was fourth down and 1 yard to go for the first down. Again Oklahoma went into a goal line defense, and again Reynolds broke clean for a touchdown. On the following kick off, Oklahoma made three first downs and then fumbled. Nebraska recovered the ball at midfield. The same pattern repeated itself. The Cornhuskers were forced into a short yardage situation. Oklahoma went into a completely forcing, goal line type defense, and once again Reynolds broke clean for a touchdown. In less than four minutes Nebraska had scored three times to go ahead 21-14.

It is possible that they might have scored the three touchdowns had Oklahoma continued to play their delaying pattern of defense. However, it would not have been possible for them to score so many points so quickly.

Since this game we have believed that our defense always should try to contain the offensive team by "defending in depth." By this we mean that the defense should be planned and played so that some member of the team always keeps outside position on the ball while other men keep all possible pass receivers in front of them.

As the ball moves down the field it becomes simpler to defend in depth since the area to be defended shrinks in size. The lateral width of the field remains the same at all times. It is a constant factor. The vertical area of field needed to be protected in depth changes with the position of the ball. When the ball is on the 50 yard line, the defensive team must defend 60 yards in depth, 50 yards to the goal line and 10 yards into the end zone. When the ball moves forward to the 20 yard line, the defensive team need defend only half as much area—20 yards to the goal line and 10 more in the end zone making the total 30 yards.

As the distance to be defended in depth shrinks, more and more members of the defensive team can be used to force the play quickly as they no longer need to drop back at the start of the play in fear of a forward pass. As the ball approaches the 10 yard line, the defense needs to defend a very small portion of the field from the standpoint of depth. At this point the containing-delaying action of the defense ceases. The entire team thinks in terms of forcing the play to prevent the touchdown.

Although many students of football will probably dispute this assumption, it is the opinion of the authors that the most difficult place on the field from which to score is first down on the 10 or 12 yard line. Here it is necessary to make as much yardage for the first down as you need to gain when on your own 20 yard line. But now the entire eleven man defensive team can concentrate their play in the 20 yard area. No men are forced to drop back to "defend in depth." When no members of the defense need to drop back, when the whole team can force the play in a relatively confined area, it is much more difficult for the offensive team to move the ball than is the case out of the field of play.

To summarize, the basic theory of defensive football should be to *contain* the offensive team and thereby prevent the single play, easy touchdown. This can be accomplished by keeping the ball always *inside* and always *in front* of the defense. When the ball is out of the field of play, some of the defense must drop back quickly with the start of each play to defend the field in depth against the long pass. As the ball moves toward the goal line, the area of the field needed to be defended in depth decreases rapidly. When the ball approaches the 10 yard line, the necessity for defending in depth no longer exists to any great degree. At this point the defense changes from the delaying theory and begins to attack. If they can successfully stop the offense in this confined area, they will have prevented the touchdown and thereby will have realized their basic objective of keeping the opponent from scoring.

4

Individual Defensive Fundamentals

The different positions on the defensive team require the execution of somewhat different techniques. However, there are certain fundamentals, common to every position, which must be mastered by all eleven players. These are:

1. The ability to move.
2. The ability to protect oneself.
3. The ability to tackle.

The most important of these fundamentals is the ability to move. Regardless of the theory or pattern of play, every defensive player must move with the snap of the ball. After his initial move, he must execute his basic assignment and protect his territory. Having done this, the individual player must move again—this time to the ball. The speed with which he moves and the accuracy of his movement will determine to a great degree his ability to play defense.

On most plays, as the ball is snapped, the offensive players attempt to block the members of the defensive team. Therefore, as a fundamental of defense every player must be able to protect himself from a block. Essentially, the ability to protect oneself means the ability to retain freedom of movement by keeping the legs free. As long as the legs are unentangled, the body can move. If the legs are controlled, the player loses the ability to move and is blocked. Thus, block protection is the ability to fight off an offensive player and retain freedom of movement.

Linemen, who are a short distance from the opposing linemen, must protect themselves at the snap of the ball. Linebackers take their positions off the line of scrimmage and have slightly more time to react before an opponent can get to them to block. Those men lined up in the deep secondary have considerable time to move before it is necessary to protect themselves.

The basic fundamentals of block protection at the time of contact are the same for all positions. As the blocker drives in to get contact, the defensive player must assume the "hitting position" and protect his legs with his shoulders, arms, and hands. The defensive man should keep his hands and arms or his shoulder between the blocker and his legs. He then can uncoil by using the muscles of his back and legs together with his shoulder and forearm to knock the blocker away from his body. This will insure his ability to maintain freedom of movement.

If a player first has the ability to move, and secondly the ability to protect himself, thus retaining his freedom of movement to the ball carrier, he then must be able to execute the fundamental of tackling. The ability to tackle effectively is the final culmination of every defensive play. If the tackle is missed, all theoretical defense, block protection, and movement to the ball will have been in vain. A good tackle involves many factors. These are:

1. In the area of contact (within 2 or 3 yards of the ball carrier), the man making the tackle must be in the "hitting position." By "hitting position" we mean that he must have a good base. His feet must be spread at least as wide as the width of his shoulders; his weight must be carried low. His eyes must be on the target. He must have enough flexing of the knees to be able to uncoil and deliver a real blow at the ball carrier. (*See Illustration No. 1.*)

2. After the player has reached the area of contact and has assumed the "hitting position," he should focus his eyes on the target. The target for the tackler should be the ball itself. Every tackler

should endeavor to drive his head through the ball. By driving the head through the ball two things are insured: First, since the ball almost always is carried on one side of the ball carrier or the other, the head will just clear the ball carrier's body when it is aimed at the ball. This will insure a solid *shoulder* instead of an *arm* tackle. Occasionally, if the head is successful in hitting the ball, the ball itself may be driven out of the ball carrier's hand by the force of the blow, and a fumble will result. In this way one of the basic objectives of defensive play may be realized— that of forcing the offense to fumble. (*See Illustration No. 2.*)

3. If the tackler has a good base, and then drives his head through the ball, he will make contact with his shoulder. As this contact is gained, the tackler should get both arms well around the ball carrier, and grab his pants or jersey. As he holds the ball carrier, he should lift him off the ground, using all of the muscles in his legs and back. As soon as the ball carrier's feet are no longer in contact with the ground, he will lose his forward drive. (*See Illustration No. 3.*)

4. At this point, the tackler will be able to drive through his opponent and throw him back to the ground. (*See Illustration No. 4.*)

A good tackle always knocks the ball carrier backward. This is the fundamental difference between a good and a poor tackle. If the defensive team allows the ball carrier to fall forward on every down, the defense almost surely will fail because, if the ball carrier is close to six feet tall, the length of his body on four successive plays will in itself almost insure the making of the first down. It is of paramount importance for the defensive team *never to let the ball carrier fall forward*. If the tackle is made as described above, and the four fundamentals of tackling are executed properly, the ball carrier will be unable to fall forward.

If each member of the defensive team is able to execute the three basic fundamentals of defensive play: (1) moving, (2) protecting himself, and (3) tackling, he is equipped, from a mechanical standpoint, to play his defensive position adequately.

In order to play intelligently, every defensive player must have a knowledge of "defensive keys." Being able to "key" properly is the essence of sound individual defensive play. A defensive key may best be described as "a movement on the part of an individual offensive player which indicates to the defensive player the direction of the offensive play." For example, if the linebacker watches the offensive guard make a pass protection block, the linebacker, keying properly, will react quickly to pass defense. The movement of the offensive guard showed that the play would be a pass before the ball was thrown. Similarly, if the offensive end blocks hard to the inside on the defensive tackle, the tackle should realize that the play will be run to his outside. By playing this key he would react quickly to the block and move to the outside. It is very easy to describe how a defensive player should react to his keys, but it is difficult to learn to react quickly and accurately.

In this respect, it should be noted that *accuracy of movement* on the part of the individual defensive player is of vital importance. If the defensive player takes one step in the wrong direction, he must take another step to regain his former position. He has already wasted two steps—is two steps late in moving in the proper direction. It is best for the defensive man to maintain his position until he is positive of the direction of the play. Then he should move to the ball carrier. He should, of course, practice diligently to increase his ability to key accurately and move quickly in the proper direction. Every player on the defensive team should have some sort of key to play instead of merely watching the ball.

Later in the book, when we discuss particular defensive alignments, we will list the keys individual players have for each defense. However, at this point it is important that each reader understand what is meant by the term "defensive keys."

In every pattern of team defense, the personnel of the team may be divided into four basic categories:

1. Linemen.
2. Linebackers.
3. Ends.
4. Secondary men.

Linemen may be identified as those defensive players who take their position within 1 yard of the line of scrimmage between the offensive ends.

Linebackers are men who line up not closer than 1 yard nor farther than 4 yards from the line of scrimmage between the offensive ends. They can drop quickly to defend against passes and move forward to stop running plays.

Ends are those men who are deployed within 1 yard of the line of scrimmage outside of the offensive end.

Secondary men are those individuals in the defensive team who are deployed at least 4 yards behind the line of scrimmage to more than 2 yards outside the offensive ends. These men have complete freedom of movement and form the basic "containing portion" of the defense.

Linemen, linebackers, ends, and secondary men must master the same three basic fundamentals to play their positions well. These fundamentals are:

Individual Defensive Fundamentals

1. Stance.
2. Reaction to the keys.
3. Movement to the ball.

FUNDAMENTALS FOR LINEMEN

The first and most important fundamental for all defensive linemen is to have a good stance. Since the offensive blocker is some 13 to 15 inches away from the defensive man, it is apparent that unless the defensive player assumes a good stance, with proper balance, he will be defeated by the blocker before he can recover his balance.

In taking his position on defense, the lineman may use either a three or four point stance. There is not much difference between the two. Either may be used effectively. However, since most teams when on offense have the linemen use a three point stance, we believe it is more simple and therefore better to use the same stance on defense. By so doing, the individual player need learn only one stance.

In taking his stance, a lineman should first drop one foot back to about the instep or heel of the opposite foot. The feet should be spread approximately the width of the shoulders or slightly wider. Weight should be equally distributed between the two feet so that balance is even between both feet and the weight is not carried too much on one side

29

or the other. Having taken the proper foot position, the individual player should do a deep-knee bend. From this position he should place his hand on the ground. If the right foot has been dropped back, the right hand should be placed on the ground. If the left foot has been dropped back, the left hand should be placed on the ground. From the deep-knee bend position, the lineman should pick out a spot just inside of the foot that is dropped back and place his hand on the ground about 3½ feet in front of that foot. The distance the hand is placed in front of the foot will vary slightly depending upon the height and physical make-up of the individual player. When the hand is placed on the ground, the hips are raised slightly until the back is almost parallel to the ground. The hand should have enough weight on it so that if it is lifted from the ground the lineman will fall forward. With this much weight forward, the defensive linemen will be able to charge forward quickly to meet the offensive blockers when the ball is snapped.

With the feet and the hand placed properly, the next essential of a good stance is proper balance. The weight should not be carried on either side; it should be equally distributed. In the same manner, the shoulders should be absolutely square to the line of scrimmage. The shoulders will be square if the hand not on the ground is in the proper position. The hand and arm not on the ground should be allowed to rest comfortably with the forearm just inside the thigh. In this manner, the hand will fall slightly inside and well forward of the knee. From this position, the hand can be moved forward quickly to protect the knee. (*See Illustrations No. 5 and 6.*)

Finally, in a good stance the head and eyes must be up. With the eyes up the player will be able to see not only the opponent in front of him, but also the opponents one man to his left and one man to his right. Since his basic key usually involves watching all three of these opponents, it is imperative that his head be up and that he develop a wide enough range of peripheral vision to see all three of his opponents.

It is vitally important that the stance of the defensive lineman enable him to be in a completely *"ready"* position. By carrying his weight well forward, the defensive man can react instantaneously with a forward movement at the snap of the ball. If the offensive players hit him before he can get in motion, he probably will be blocked. On the other hand, if he can react quickly and be moving at the time of contact, it will be much easier for him to maintain freedom of movement and avoid the block.

Illustrations 5 and 6 show a good defensive line

stance from in front and from the side. Notice how the weight is evenly balanced on both feet, how the back is almost parallel to the ground, how much of the weight is carried by the hand on the ground, and how ready the player is to charge forward instantaneously.

The *key* for any defensive lineman is the movement of the offensive men in his area. An interior lineman will always have three offensive men to watch—the man in front of him and the offensive players to his right and left. A lineman who is playing so wide that he is in the area of the offensive end may have only the end and the tackle to watch. Nevertheless, the key remains the same. It is the movement of the offensive men in his area.

As the ball is snapped, the defensive lineman should start his charge forward. As he makes this first movement, which is basically an uncoiling of the legs and body, he should watch carefully the movements of the men opposite him. His charge usually is directed at the opponent immediately in front of him, but as he moves on this course, he watches the men on either side. If the man at his left drives in on him, he should throw as much of the power of his charge as possible at that opponent. If, on the other hand, the opponent at his right charges in on him, he should divert his charge in that direction.

If neither of these men charge at him, he should continue on his original course at the opponent directly in front of him. He should hit the opponent hard enough to force him back away from his body and thereby maintain his freedom of movement.

Defensive linemen can protect themselves with either of two basic charges. These charges are: (1) hand shiver and (2) forearm shiver. There is a great deal of controversy among football coaches as to which of these defensive charges is the better. Both are good. We do not believe it is fair to say one is better than the other. Under normal circumstances, the shorter, more compact man will probably be more effective using the hand shiver because he will be short enough to use his hands forcefully and still not stand so high that his legs are vulnerable for a block. When a man has strength in this position, the hand shiver is undoubtedly the best charge because contact with his hands will always keep the opponent farther from his legs than is possible when using his forearms. (*See Illustrations No. 7 and 8.*)

However, when the defensive player is tall and slender, it will probably be very difficult for him to get low enough to operate with strength while using the hand shiver. If he fails to catch the offensive man with his hands, the opponent will penetrate quickly to his body and legs, and the defensive man will lose

33

his freedom of movement. Therefore, a tall man is usually better off using the forearm shiver.

In the forearm shiver, one arm or the other is used to hit the offensive man, to raise him up and keep him away from the defensive player's body and legs. Forearms have a great deal more surface than do the hands. They can be used with strength very close to the ground.

The hand shiver, when used, should be executed in the following manner: The defensive lineman should take a short step forward with the foot that he has dropped back. As this foot is placed on the ground, which means that both feet are on the ground at the same time, the body should be uncoiled quickly and the hands and arms shot forward with a sharp, pressing motion. The heels of the hands should be aimed at a spot just under the shoulders of the offensive blocker. After hitting the target, the hands should be driven forward and up so that the offensive player is raised as his charge is stopped. This will leave the center of gravity of the defensive man lower than the offensive player's and it will be easy for him to force the offensive player away from his body. The defensive player is now free to knock his opponent backwards, and at the same time to maintain his balance and his ability to move laterally.

The forearm shiver is employed in much the same

34

Illustration No. 5. Good defensive line stance: front view.

Illustration No. 6. Good defensive line stance: side view.

Illustration No. 7. Hand-shiver charge: view at point of contact.

Illustration No. 8. Forearm-shiver charge: view at point of contact.

Illustration No. 9. Three-on-one defensive group drill.

Illustration No. 10. Five-on-three defensive group drill.

Illustration No. 11. Five-on-five defensive group drill.

Illustration No. 12. Stance of defensive linebacker: front view.

Illustration No. 13. Stance of defensive linebacker: side view.

manner although it is usually delivered with only one arm rather than with both hands. The strongest type of forearm shiver usually comes from the hand which is on the ground as the ball is snapped. Again the lineman's feet will move just as they did in the hand shiver. The rear foot should be brought up until it is approximately even with the other foot. This will leave both feet on the ground and parallel to the line of scrimmage. As this short step is taken the player's body should be uncoiled and the hand on the ground should be raised up and out with as much force as possible. The target for the forearm is the spot just below the numerals on the offensive man's jersey. The opposite hand should endeavor to drive underneath the shoulder about as described for the hand shiver. If proper contact is made, the forearm should follow through, raise the opponent up and drive him back. Again the defensive player will be in position to control the offensive man and move laterally to the ball.

The basic objective of both of these charges is to control one's own territory while maintaining the ability to move laterally. In sequence, the fundamentals for any defensive charge are as follows: (1) charge with the snap of the ball, (2) protect yourself, (3) protect your territory, (4) move to the ball, and (5) make the tackle.

35

If he has the proper stance, the lineman will always be able to charge when the ball is snapped. By using the hand shiver or the forearm shiver, the defensive player should be able to defeat the charge of his offensive opponent and protect his territory. If he is able to handle the opponent in front of him, he will have retained his freedom of movement. Remember, the essential objective of both the forearm and the hand shiver charge is to keep the opponent away from the defensive man's body so that his legs remain free, and he retains his ability to move. After defeating the blocker in front of him and protecting his own territory, the defensive lineman must move to the ball with all possible speed.

DRILLS TO TEACH FUNDAMENTAL DEFENSIVE LINE PLAY

I. *Learning to take the proper stance.* A good stance is so much a matter of personal balance, governed by the physical build of the individual, that there seems to be no other way of teaching it than to have the coach instruct each man individually on how to take his position. He should then watch each man take a stance several times to be sure that it is taken properly. It is usually necessary to check each man every day. By so doing the players well learn the importance of having a good stance all of the time and will soon develop the habit of lining up properly.

II. *Development of forearm or hand shiver*. After having learned to assume a good stance, the defensive player should concentrate on developing the strength of his hands or arms as used in making his defensive charge. This can be accomplished by placing a dummy approximately two feet from the defensive player. A teammate should hold the dummy. On the snap of the ball (or a starting signal), the defensive player should step forward with his rear foot, bringing it up on line with the forward foot as he uncoils his legs and body. He should hit the dummy with as much force as possible, using the forearm or hand shiver. This charge must be delivered with enough power to knock the dummy back while the feet remain far enough behind the dummy to avoid getting tangled up. *Remember,* the most important feature of the defensive charge is to knock the opponent *away from* the defensive man thereby leaving the defensive player's legs free so that he may move to the ball.

As soon as the defensive man has mastered this charge, he should be placed in a "man on man" situation. In this drill an offensive man is placed opposite a defensive man. At the snap of the ball, the offensive man tries to block; the defensive man, using the forearm or hand shiver, charges and attempts to defeat the opponent.

After a defensive player has learned to handle one offensive man, he should be put in a "3 on 1" situation. This drill approximates quite closely the situation he actually will face under game conditions. The coach should stand behind the three offensive men and indicate which man is supposed to make the block. A ball carrier may be used but it perhaps is better in this drill to have the defensive man react entirely to the three linemen who comprise his key instead of looking into the back field to watch the

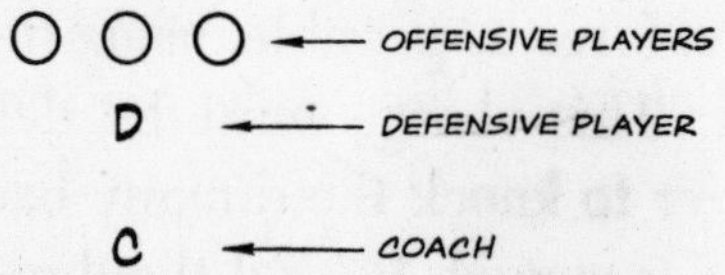

O O O ——— OFFENSIVE PLAYERS

D ——— DEFENSIVE PLAYER

C ——— COACH

SETUP FOR THE THREE-ON-ONE DRILL

Figure 1

ball carrier. The three offensive linemen have five plays: (1) they may put on a double team block from the left, (2) they may double team from the right, (3) the man in front of the defensive player may block him to the left while the other men pull out and run in that direction, (4) he may block to the right while his teammates pull in that direction, and (5) all three men may drop back executing a pass protection block. (*See Illustration No. 9.*)

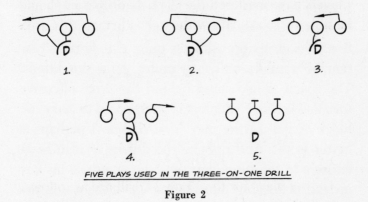

1.   2.   3.

4.   5.

FIVE PLAYS USED IN THE THREE-ON-ONE DRILL

Figure 2

The coach stands behind the defensive player and indicates which of the five basic movements the offensive men are to use. He then gives the snap signal, and the play proceeds under full-speed, game-like conditions. The defensive player soon learns to react quickly to his key, and while reacting to his key, learns to protect himself as has been described above.

As soon as the individual defensive players have mastered the "3 on 1" drill, they are ready to proceed to the "5 on 2" drill. This drill is set up with five offensive linemen and two defensive players. The two defensive players play opposite the two and four men on the offensive line. They react exactly as they

39

do for the "3 on 1" drill. Each defensive man watches the three opponents in his area. If the defensive players have mastered the "3 on 1" drill, they should be able to coordinate with each other on this drill.

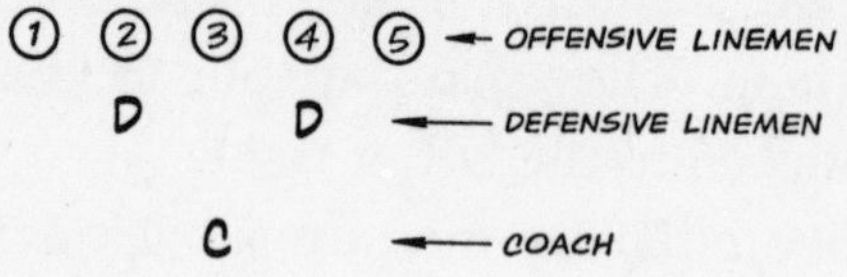

①　②　③　④　⑤　←— OFFENSIVE LINEMEN

D　　　D　　←——— DEFENSIVE LINEMEN

C　　　←——— COACH

SETUP FOR THE FIVE-ON-TWO DRILL

Figure 3

The six plays for the "5 on 2" drill are as follows:

1. The offensive No. 3 and No. 4 men double team the defensive player while the No. 1 man moves into the secondary and the No. 2 man pulls as an "influence" in an effort to get the defensive player to follow him. The No. 5 man then traps the other defensive lineman.

2. (This is the same play run in the opposite direction.) The No. 2 and No. 3 men double team. The No. 4 and No. 5 men "influence" and the No. 1 man traps.

3. The No. 1 and No. 2 men double team and the No. 4 man single blocks as the No. 3 and No. 5 men pull to the defensive left.

4. (This is the same as Play 3 run in the opposite direction.) The No. 4 and No. 5 men double team.

40

No. 2 man single blocks and Nos. 1 and 3 pull to the defensive right.

5. This is a single blocking play where the No. 1, No. 3, and No. 5 men go straight down the field while the No. 2 and No. 4 men block the opponents opposite them. They may be split as diagrammed or both blocked to the left or right.

6. All five offensive men drop back and make a pass protection block.

After practicing the "3 on 1" drill, and the "5 on 2" drill, without a backfield man, it is well to use a ball

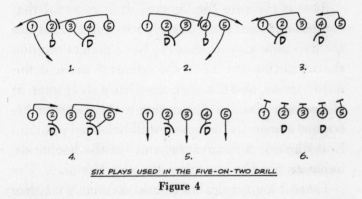

SIX PLAYS USED IN THE FIVE-ON-TWO DRILL

Figure 4

carrier so that the coach can be sure the defensive players are keying properly—watching the linemen— and not looking into the backfield. Surprising as it may seem, most defensive players react very well to the blocks of the offensive men *which are actually their keys* when no ball carrier is used in the drill.

As soon as a ball carrier is added they neglect to watch the offensive blocking. They concentrate on looking at the ball carrier, forget their keys, and thereby become vulnerable to the blockers.

A "5 on 3" or a "5 on 5" drill can also be used. The same pattern of plays described for the "5 on 2" drill are executed by the offensive men; while the defensive players learn to react from slightly different alignments. (*See Illustrations No. 10 and 11.*)

FUNDAMENTALS FOR LINEBACKERS

As was the case for linemen, it is essential that defensive linebackers have a good stance. It is not quite so necessary for them to be in perfect position as it is for linemen since the offensive blockers are farther away, and the linebacker has a short interval of time after the ball is snapped to recover from his original stance and assume a well-balanced position. Nevertheless, it is advantageous for the linebacker to have a good stance when the play begins.

There is a great deal of discussion among coaches as to which foot should be dropped back by the linebacker in his stance. Most players, as they move forward, tend habitually to move either the right or the left foot. In coaching the linebacker, we believe his stance should be adapted to this tendency. Since most men are right handed, they will usually drop their right foot back and move the right foot first when starting forward. Thus, it is best for most men to take their stance with the right foot back about on a line with the heel of the left foot. The feet should be spread approximately the width of the shoulders. The knees should be flexed and the body bent slightly at the waist. The arms should be allowed to hang straight down and should be carried very loosely. Shoulders should be parallel to the line of scrimmage. The linebacker must look intently at his key, which, in most instances, will be one offensive lineman. (*See Illustrations No. 12 and 13.*)

The movement of this offensive lineman will indicate to the linebacker the direction and type of play. The offensive lineman always makes one of six basic moves. He either: (1) charges straight at the linebacker, (2) blocks hard at the lineman to his left, (3) blocks hard at the lineman to his right, (4) pulls

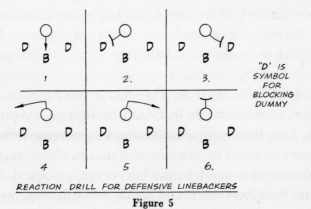

REACTION DRILL FOR DEFENSIVE LINEBACKERS

Figure 5

to the left, (5) pulls to the right, or (6) drops back and makes a pass-protection block.

The linebacker should react to each key as follows: (1) If the lineman charges him, he should move in to meet the lineman, hit him, control him, force him back, and thereby retain his ability to move laterally. (2) If the lineman blocks aggressively either to his right or to his left, the linebacker should shoot the gap. (3) If the lineman pulls to either side, the linebacker should go with him. (4) If the lineman makes a pass-protection block, the linebacker should drop quickly to the hook-pass zone.

If the linebacker can learn to make these moves quickly and accurately as the offensive lineman moves, if he does not "false step," or worse still step in the wrong direction, he will be in position to support almost every play.

As the linebacker reacts to his keys and starts to move to the ball, he will be blocked by some member of the offensive team. In protecting himself, he should use either the hand shiver or the forearm shiver charge in the same way as was described previously for linemen. This charge can never be as clean or accurate as that used by linemen because the linebacker will, almost always, be moving before he is contacted by the offensive player. However, in the area of contact, as the linebacker is blocked, he must make every effort to assume the hitting position. He must lower his center of gravity, flex his knees, and hit his opponent with the forearm or hand shiver. The blow should be delivered from underneath his opponent and should raise him up and drive him back and away from the linebacker's body so that he is free to continue his movement to the ball. (*See Illustration No. 14.*)

In learning to play the position, certain drills should be used. Again, the first fundamental is to learn the proper stance. This can be done as was described for linemen. Each individual must be coached in his stance until he knows how to line up properly.

Learning to "key" is simply a matter of practice in reacting to the movement of one offensive player. This can be best taught by two linebackers working together. Two dummies should be placed on either side of the man who will simulate the offensive player. These dummies will take the place of two defensive linemen. The linebacker then takes his stance about five feet away from the offensive player. The offensive player then moves very quickly in one of the six courses described above. The linebacker must move smoothly and accurately in response to this key. (*See Figure 5.*)

As soon as the linebacker learns to move with his key, the drill should be done under scrimmage conditions. At this point a ball carrier is deployed behind the offensive player. Dummies are spread out along the line of scrimmage in positions corresponding to those taken by the defensive linemen. As the ball is

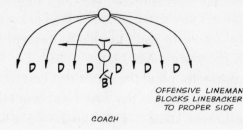

OFFENSIVE LINEMAN
BLOCKS LINEBACKER
TO PROPER SIDE

COACH

LINEBACKER REACTION DRILL NO. 2

Figure 6

snapped, the offensive player blocks or pulls and leads in the proper direction full speed against the linebacker. The ball carrier runs between the dummies in any one of the six courses indicated. The linebacker must now react quickly to the blocker and ball carrier. He must make the tackle as the ball carrier runs through the hole indicated by the coach. Occasionally, the blocker should make a pass-protection block, and the ball carrier should drop back to throw. If the linebacker can avoid the block, drop back quickly to play pass defense, move accurately to the correct hole, and then tackle the ball carrier as he hits the hole, he will have completely mastered the fundamentals of his position.

FUNDAMENTALS FOR THE PLAY
OF DEFENSIVE ENDS

The stance of the defensive end can be either the three-point position taken by defensive linemen or the upright stance used by a linebacker.

The end on defense will have approximately the same amount of reaction time on most defenses as does the linebacker. There is one essential difference between the play of the ends and linebackers. The linebacker "keys" and then moves while the end moves as he "keys."

There is no single perfect key for the defensive end. Variations in the pattern used by the offensive backfield make it virtually impossible for the end to take his cue from any one man in the backfield. Watching two or more backs can be done, but it is reasonably difficult. The best key for ends seems to be that of playing the ball.

The end should take one step across the line of scrimmage as the ball is snapped and key the ball as follows:

1. If the ball is coming his way, he will continue in, meet the blockers, and force the play.

2. If the ball is going away from him, he will drop back quickly and become a secondary man.

3. If the ball moves back away from the line of scrimmage for a pass, the end will drop back quickly

to his outside to become a pass defender (This information is covered in detail in Chapter 6).

The fundamental play of the end in the area of contact is almost exactly the same as that for the defensive linebacker. When the ball comes his way, he must meet the blockers on balance with a good forearm or hand shiver. He must never let them get to his legs and must maintain his freedom of movement. It goes without saying that it is necessary for him to learn the fundamental execution of tackling as well as the fundamental defensive block protection as stated above.

FUNDAMENTALS FOR SECONDARY MEN

The stance of the secondary men is not as vital as it is for linemen, linebackers or ends since secondary men are so far away from the offensive team that they have plenty of time to recover their balance before a defensive player can get to their area. However, it is well that they learn to take a stance with their feet spread approximately the width of the shoulders and with their knees slightly flexed. They should have the same perfect balance at the time the ball is snapped as a good baseball infielder has at the moment the ball is pitched.

Having taken a good stance, the defensive secondary man should look intently at his key. There is no single, sure key for defensive secondary men as constant and as foolproof as the keys for a lineman or linebacker. In most instances, if the defensive secondary men will look through the offensive linemen who are *uncovered* to the backfield, they will be playing the best key available.

By "uncovered offensive linemen," we mean those men in the offensive line who do not have a defensive lineman opposite them on the line of scrimmage. These men will be free to move at the start of the play. They will give the best tip-off to the defensive secondary as to whether the play is a run or a pass. If the uncovered lineman crosses the line of scrimmage and comes downfield the play must be a run. If the uncovered lineman does *not* cross the line of scrimmage, the play could develop into a pass and must be played accordingly.

Whether the play is a pass or a run is the basic, essential problem that must be solved by the defensive secondary men. In every instance, the men in the secondary should *play every play as a pass* until it can no longer be a pass play. There is only one movement on the part of the offensive team which completely eliminates the possibility of the forward pass. If the line of scrimmage is crossed by the guards, tackles, or center of the offensive team the play cannot be a pass because ineligible men are downfield.

If the defensive secondary men will look through the uncovered offensive linemen, they will get a reasonably quick key as soon as the play starts as to whether it is a pass or a run. If the uncovered linemen cross the line of scrimmage and come down field, the secondary men should *come up and play for a run* because the offensive team no longer can throw the ball. The rules prohibit them from so doing. On the other hand, if the offensive linemen do not come down field, if they all stay behind the line of scrimmage, the defensive secondary men should drop back and play against a possible forward pass. They can never be sure the play will not develop into a pass unless a lineman has crossed the line of scrimmage or the ball has crossed the line of scrimmage.

Most long forward-pass touchdowns result from defensive secondary men coming up quickly because they believe a running play has started when actually the play is a pass. By watching the uncovered lineman, by playing pass until the linemen are down the field, or until the ball itself has crossed the line of scrimmage, the defensive secondary men should be able to prevent any long passes from being completed behind them.

As the defensive secondary man comes up to stop the running play (when his key indicates the play will be a run), he should use the same fundamental block protection to maintain his freedom of move-

Illustration No. 14. Defensive linebacker meeting blocker.

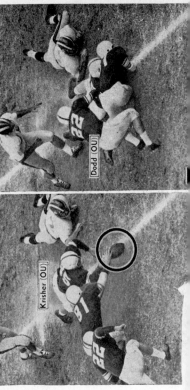

Illustration No. 15. Stunting lineman, Bill Krisher, causes a fumble, which is recovered by the University of Oklahoma.

ment as was described for the linebackers. In the area of contact he should use the essentials of the forearm shiver or the hand shiver.

SUMMARY

In building a house, the first essential for a sound structure is a good foundation. The same theory is true in building a good football team. Regardless of the pattern of defensive play, regardless of the deployment of individual defensive men, the basic essential upon which the defense must depend will be sound fundamental play on the part of the individual men of the defensive team. All defensive men must be able to move, all defensive men must be able to protect themselves, and all defensive men must be able to tackle.

Within the pattern of defense being played, there will always be defensive linemen, defensive linebackers, defensive ends, and defensive secondary men. All four groups must have a good stance. They must all key accurately to the movement of the players of the offensive team. They must use a defensive charge in the area of contact which will maintain their ability to defend themselves and to move to the ball. As they get to the ball, they must be able to make the tackle. A team that can execute the basic fundamentals described above will be able to play well from almost any defensive alignment.

5

The Two Distinct Units of the Defensive Team

As has been stated previously, the most important mission of the defense is to prevent the one play, easy touchdown. In order to do this it is necessary that certain individuals of the defensive team play with only one objective in mind—to stop the one play, breakaway touchdown. This group of defensive personnel is known as the "containing portion" of the defense.

Those men not used in the containing portion of the defense, comprise the "forcing" portion of the defense. Their mission is to attack, with the snap of the ball, in an effort to get to the ball carrier on or behind the line of scrimmage. If they are successful, the play will be held to a short gain or thrown for a loss. If they fail completely, they will be backed up by the containing unit and a medium gain, rather than a touchdown, will result.

52

Two Distinct Units of Defensive Team

The numbers of men involved in the containing portion of the defense will vary depending upon the alignment being used. However, the basic assignment of the containing portion of the defense remains the same. It is *always to keep the ball in front of them and inside of them.*

If they are successful in executing this assignment, it goes without saying that it will be impossible for the offensive team ever to make a breakaway touchdown.

This assignment should *never* be varied at any time. If any member of the containing portion of the defense ever comes up too quickly to support a running play, or commits himself too quickly in an attempt to knock down a short or a flat pass, he will be vulnerable to a breakaway play. In order to execute their assignment without error, the containing portion of the defense should have only the one assignment. No variations should ever be allowed. In this way, the chance of errors will be reduced. If all mistakes in this area can be avoided, the prime purpose of defense—that of preventing the easy touchdown—will have been accomplished by the containing unit of the defensive team.

The theory of play of the forcing portion of the defense is exactly opposite that of the containing. From an assignment standpoint, it is their mission to *force an error* on the part of the offensive team. If they cannot force an error, they should try to charge hard enough, and penetrate quickly enough, to get to the ball carrier at the line of scrimmage or behind it so that he will not be able to pick up a succession of short gains and thereby make a series of first downs. In the same manner, they must rush the passer hard enough to make it difficult for him to throw accurately.

Since the forcing portion of the defense is backed up by the firm control of the containing unit, they can gamble in an effort to accomplish the purposes stated above. It is possible for the forcing portion of the defense to use a number of widely varied alignments and, by changing the spacing between men and their angle of charge, to force an assignment error on the part of the offensive team.

Whenever a defensive unit uses a great number of alignments, it is possible that they themselves will make a mistake. Naturally, every effort should be made to avoid errors. But if the containing unit functions properly, an error on the part of the forcing unit will result in only a 10, 12, or 15 yard gain because the containing group will always back up, and support the forcing unit. This fact gives the forcing unit complete freedom of play. They know that they will be backed up and supported one hundred per cent of the time by the containing unit.

The most difficult assignment for the forcing unit of the defense is to pursue accurately. The so-called "angle of pursuit" is a phrase popularized by one of football's all-time great coaches, Colonel Earl (Red) Blaik of West Point. The "angle of pursuit" simply means that each man in the forcing portion of the defense, after protecting his territory, should move at an angle to put himself in front of the ball at the earliest possible moment. Obviously, a wide variety of angles will result for each individual as the ball moves in the many directions it does in various plays. Two factors are involved in an individual's moving on the proper angle of pursuit: (1) the speed of the ball carrier, and (2) the speed of the pursuer. A fast ball carrier will obviously get to the point of attack quicker than a slow one. The same thing is true concerning the speed of the defensive man. These factors cause the proper angle of pursuit to vary for each man on almost every play.

By constant practice and application, defensive players can be taught to move on the proper angle since one factor remains constant—their own speed. At the start of each play they charge and protect their territory. Having done so, they pick up the movement of the ball carrier, judge his speed, and begin to move at that angle which will put them in front of the ball carrier at the earliest possible moment.

If the forcing portion of the defensive team pursues accurately, they will always be in position to support the containing part of the defense as they move in to stop the play. It is difficult for any one man to make a clean tackle—that is in what amounts to a relatively open field when a "1 on 1" situation evolves between the ball carrier and the tackler. This is particularly true when the ball carrier has ample room to maneuver. The advantage in this instance is all with the ball carrier. However, a team using the proper angle of pursuit will almost always catch the ball carrier, who has been slowed down in his efforts to avoid a single tackler.

To summarize, each defensive team is made up of two basic units, the "containing portion" of the defensive team and the "forcing portion" of the defensive team. The forcing portion, as the term implies, makes every effort to settle the issue immediately with the offensive team in the sure knowledge that they will be supported one hundred per cent by the solid wall of the containing unit.

It is always possible to prevent the long pass and the long touchdown run if the forcing portion can be taught to react quickly on the proper angle of pursuit after each man has protected his own territory. By pursuing properly they will come to the immediate assistance of the containing man who attempts the open field tackle and will be in position to support him if he fails to make the play.

6

Play of the Containing Portion of the Defensive Team

In discussing the play of the containing portion of the defense, we will assume for the time being that the offensive team is in a balanced offensive formation without flankers or men in motion. The same plan of defense is applied when the formation becomes unbalanced as is a single wing or a "T" formation with flankers. The theory can be explained more simply and perhaps understood more readily if we consider it first against a straight, balanced offensive setup.

The containing portion of the defense can be likened to a wheel.

Consider the ball as the hub of a wheel and the players assigned to the containing portion of the defense as the ends of the spokes of the wheel. When these spokes are hypothetically connected, they will form a rim for the wheel. The rim of the wheel, extended, surrounds the entire offensive team. Every man on the offense is in front of and inside of the rim of the wheel formed by the containing unit.

In action, the containing men coordinate and play together as they would if they actually were attached to a wheel. If the ball starts to the defense's left, the wheel simply turns to the left. If the ball moves to the right, the wheel turns in that direction. If the ball moves straight ahead quickly, the rim of the wheel shrinks. If the passer drops back to throw, the wheel quickly enlarges.

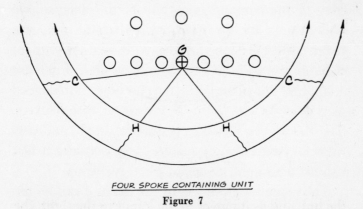

FOUR SPOKE CONTAINING UNIT

Figure 7

The concept of using the wheel as the example for the movement of the containing portion of the defense seems to enable each player to picture in his mind and thereby grasp more easily the necessary coordination between himself and his teammates.

When a 4-man containing unit is used, there will be four spokes in the wheel. The two corner men and the two deep safeties make up the spokes.

The five-spoke wheel with five men involved in the containing portion of the defense operates in exactly the same manner. The ball again is the hub of the wheel. Five men, the two ends and the three deep-backs, comprise the spokes. Imagine the rim of the wheel connecting these five players. The ball is

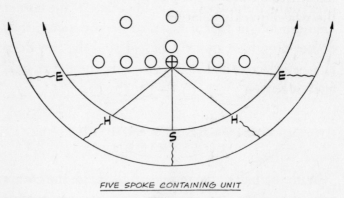

FIVE SPOKE CONTAINING UNIT

Figure 8

the hub and as it moves to the left or to the right, the wheel turns in that direction to keep the ball inside of the containing men. If the ball moves back away from the line of scrimmage, the spokes get longer, the rim enlarges, and all offensive men are kept in front of the containing portion of the defense.

PLAY OF THE FOUR-SPOKE CONTAINING UNIT

We will assume that the ball is in the middle field. The four spoke unit is made up of two corner men and two deep halfbacks. All four men must realize that this is a *four deep* defense, not a *two deep* defense. With this thought in mind, the corner men will realize that they must drop back quickly to keep everything in front of and inside them. If the corner men are taught that it is a two deep defense, they do not drop back quickly enough and the two deep men will have difficulty in covering the entire field against passes.

ASSIGNMENTS FOR THE CORNER MEN

With the ball in the middle of the field, the corner men should line up approximately 4 yards outside the offensive end, and 4 yards behind the line of scrimmage. (This position will vary with the lateral field position of the ball as will be explained later in the chapter on pass defense.) From this position, the corner men will take the stance of defense secondary men. They should key the movement of the ball, or if possible, the one man in the offensive back field who gives them the best indication as to the direction and pattern of the play. Since most teams do not have a reliable tip-off from the movement of any one man in the back field, the easiest, best, most accurate key seems to be that of playing the movement of the ball itself.

Essentially, the corner men play as ends following the simple adage "Ball come, I come; ball go, I go."

A more detailed explanation of this simple phrase is that if the ball starts toward the corner man he should give ground with it, moving laterally toward the sidelines. As he makes this move, he should look through the uncovered lineman on the offensive team. If that lineman comes down field, the corner man should immediately come up to turn the play in. However, if the ineligible pass receiver does not cross the line of scrimmage, the corner man should continue to move laterally three or four steps and then drop back. If the corner man is sure the play will be a run and decides to come up, he should force the play, meet the blockers, retain outside position on the ball, stay on his feet, and at all costs turn the ball to the inside. If he is *not sure* the play is a run and is of the opinion that a pass may be developing, he should drop quickly to cover the deep outside zone. (A more detailed explanation of pass defense will be given in Chapter 18.)

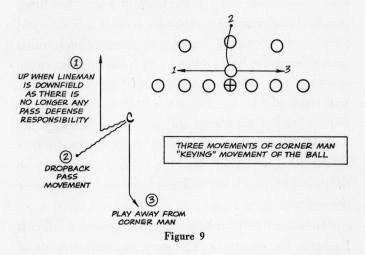

THREE MOVEMENTS OF CORNER MAN
"KEYING" MOVEMENT OF THE BALL

① UP WHEN LINEMAN IS DOWNFIELD AS THERE IS NO LONGER ANY PASS DEFENSE RESPONSIBILITY

② DROPBACK PASS MOVEMENT

③ PLAY AWAY FROM CORNER MAN

Figure 9

If, when the play starts, the ball goes away from the corner man, he should drop straight back downfield, again watching the movement of the offensive line. If linemen are coming downfield, which indicates that the play no longer can possibly develop into a pass, the corner man should move across the field at a slight angle while maintaining outside position on the ball. By this movement he becomes the safety man against all plays moving to the opposite side.

If, as he starts to drop back, no movement of an offensive lineman indicates that the play will be a

63

run, he should continue to drop absolutely straight back. If he is sure that all eleven offensive men are inside of him, he may angle slightly across the field, but he must remain constantly alert for a delayed pass receiver moving "against the grain" back to his area. When the ball moves away from him, he is the deep outside defender against all passes.

If the ball does not move to either side, but simply moves back away from the line of scrimmage for a drop back pass, the corner man again follows through his maxim of "Ball go, I go." In this case, he drops back quickly on an angle back and out to cover the outside deep zone.

Adjustments to flankers sometimes poses a difficult problem for the coach. The play and adjustments of the four-spoke containing unit should be varied so the offense can be kept off balance. However, the basic rules for adjustment to flankers on the part of

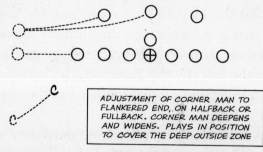

ADJUSTMENT OF CORNER MAN TO FLANKERED END, ON HALFBACK OR FULLBACK. CORNER MAN DEEPENS AND WIDENS. PLAYS IN POSITION TO COVER THE DEEP OUTSIDE ZONE

Figure 10

the corner men are as follows: (1) If the end is a flanker to your side, deepen and be in position to cover him if he goes straight down the field as the widest eligible pass receiver. (2) If the "on halfback" (that is, the halfback on your side) flankers to your side, drop out and cover him exactly as you would a flankered end. (3) If the fullback flankers to the side of the corner man, drop back and cover him exactly as you would the flankered end. Concerning a flankered end on halfback or fullback flankered, the corner man always drops off and out and covers in the same manner. (4) If the opposite halfback crosses to the side of the corner man, the corner man should come up and play as a defensive end. The remaining three men will rotate to compensate for

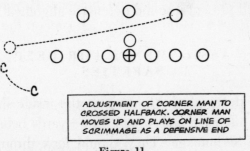

ADJUSTMENT OF CORNER MAN TO CROSSED HALFBACK. CORNER MAN MOVES UP AND PLAYS ON LINE OF SCRIMMAGE AS A DEFENSIVE END

Figure 11

this adjustment. (5) If the halfback on the corner man's side crosses to the opposite side, the corner

65

man will drop back and play exactly as a wide safety of a five-man containing unit.

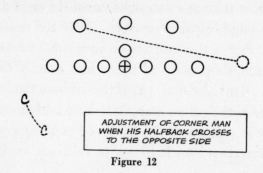

ADJUSTMENT OF CORNER MAN
WHEN HIS HALFBACK CROSSES
TO THE OPPOSITE SIDE

Figure 12

These rules must be adjusted slightly depending on lateral field positions and the most dangerous plays of the offensive team. However, under normal circumstances, these simple rules, when applied by the corner men in making adjustments to the flankers, will present a sound defensive alignment.

ASSIGNMENTS FOR DEEP SAFETIES

The deep safeties line up on the inside shoulder of the offensive ends about 8 to 9 yards behind the line of scrimmage They should look through the uncovered lineman to the ball. If "odd" spacing is being used the deep safeties will look through the guards to the ball. If "even" spacing is being used, they should look through the center or tackle to the ball.

There is seldom a foolproof backfield or end key for these men. Most offenses are organized in such a

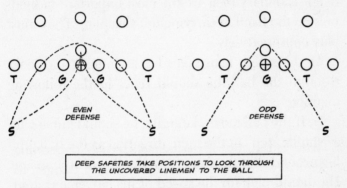

Figure 13

manner that trying to key any particular individual at end or in the backfield can be extremely dangerous and lead to a bad error. Therefore, it is best for these men to key the uncovered linemen as they move with the ball. *They should play pass on every play until the uncovered lineman crosses the line of scrimmage and comes downfield.* When this occurs, the offense cannot throw the ball legally. Since the play will be a run, the safety men can come up.

If the lineman does *not* come downfield, the deep safeties should always play pass *until the ball carrier crosses the line of scrimmage.*

This may seem an unduly conservative type of play. Perhaps it is. However, as was pointed out previously, this theory of defense is based entirely on avoiding the one play, cheap, easy touchdown. The deep secondary men are the most important individuals on the team in carrying out this plan. They must play conservatively.

As the safety man takes his alignment and looks through the ball, he should react in the following manner:

1. If the ball moves laterally, he should move with a "shuffle step" in the same direction as the ball, giving ground slightly away from the line of scrimmage. He should pick up the speed of his movement gradually and should continue to move laterally and slightly backward as the ball moves laterally. When the ball stops moving laterally, the ball carrier will be turned up the field on a running play or the ball carrier will have stopped and set himself to throw a forward pass. The key of the linemen should help the deep safety in his decision as to which of these alternatives will occur. The important adjustment, however, is that of *stopping* lateral movement as soon as the ball stops moving toward the sideline.

As he stops his lateral movement, the safety, if a pass is developing, should drop straight back. If a run is developing, he should come up to support.

2. If the ball goes to the side away from the deep safety, he should again start his movement with the "shuffle step," but should deepen more quickly than he does when the ball moves to his side. Except for this one slight variation, he should react exactly as he would if the ball were coming to his side.

3. When the ball moves straight ahead on a quick opening drive, the deep safety will probably not be in position to support too quickly since he will, at the snap of the ball, take his same regular "shuffle step." On the quick play to his side, if the lineman's key indicates the play cannot be a pass, he should come up and support. If the quick play is to the opposite side, he will be dropping back and will become a second safety should the first safety miss the tackle.

4. When a drop back pass develops, the safety man again will move with his same "shuffle step" and will drop back to cover the deep field on his side. This movement will be described in more detail in the chapter on pass defense.

ADJUSTMENTS TO FLANKERS— DEEP SAFETIES

The Deep Safety has four simple assignments in making his adjustments to flankers.

1. If the on halfback (halfback on his side) or the fullback flankers to his side, the deep safety makes

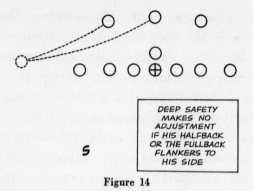

Figure 14

no adjustment. He retains his position in relation to the offensive end and reacts to the movement of the ball exactly as he would against the balanced formation without flankers.

2. If the offensive end flankers, the deep safety maintains his position and again reacts to the movement of the ball exactly as he would against the reg-

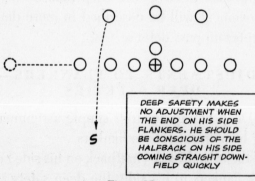

Figure 15

ular "T." However, he should be aware when the end flankers that the halfback on his side can get downfield very quickly. He should be conscious of the halfback as the play begins.

3. The only real adjustment for the deep safety will be against crossed halfbacks. When the *opposite halfback crosses to the side of the deep safety*, the corner man will be rotated up (as was stated previously). Therefore, the deep safety must move over with the flanker and play deep enough and wide enough to cover the deep outside zone at all times. He should take his position approximately 8 yards away from the flanker (regardless of the depth of the flanker behind the line of scrimmage) and should be slightly on the flanker's outside unless the flanker is closer than 8 yards to the sidelines. If the flanker is this close to the sidelines, the safety should play inside of him. When the ball is snapped, he will

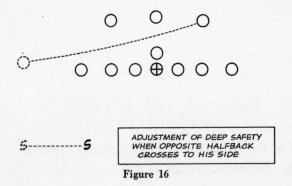

ADJUSTMENT OF DEEP SAFETY
WHEN OPPOSITE HALFBACK
CROSSES TO HIS SIDE

Figure 16

71

play exactly as would the wide safety of a five man containing unit.

4. When the offensive *halfback on the side of the deep safety crosses to the opposite side,* the deep safety on that side will be widening. Therefore, the other safety must move over to cover the deep middle zone. In making this adjustment, the deep safety should line up approximately on the offensive guard or tackle to the side of the flanker about 8 to 10 yards from the line of scrimmage. He will react normally from this position as would the middle safety of a five man containing unit.

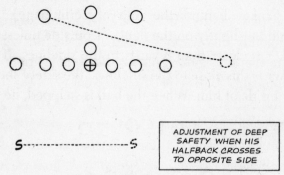

ADJUSTMENT OF DEEP
SAFETY WHEN HIS
HALFBACK CROSSES
TO OPPOSITE SIDE

Figure 17

PLAY OF THE FIVE-SPOKE CONTAINING UNIT

The five-spoke containing defense operates in exactly the same manner as the four-spoke.

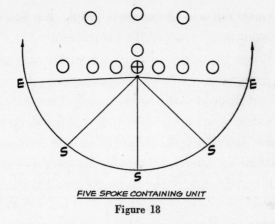

FIVE SPOKE CONTAINING UNIT

Figure 18

PLAY OF THE ENDS—
FIVE-SPOKE DEFENSE

The play of the ends of the five-spoke defense corresponds almost exactly to that of the two corner men in the four-spoke defense. Both ends apply the same maxim, "Ball come, I come; ball go, I go."

If the ball starts towards the end, he should cross the line quickly, fight off the blockers coming at him, and retain his ability to move to the outside so that the ball cannot get around him. It is important in this instance that the end move almost straight across the line of scrimmage. If he moves straight across, he does not have too radical an angle of adjustment to give ground to the outside to keep the ball from getting around him. By lining up only 1½

73

to 2 yards outside the offensive end, the defensive man can cross the line at the proper angle.

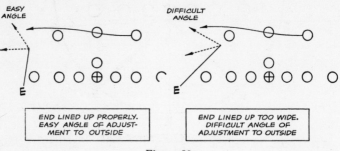

Figure 19

If the defense player lines up 3 to 4 yards outside of the offensive end, and when the ball starts towards him, comes across the line at a sharp angle to the inside to meet the play, he will have a very acute angle of adjustment to the outside to keep the ball from getting around him. This is a most difficult maneuver for him. If the end charges on a sharp inside angle, and the ball carrier gives ground, the end may lose leverage and let the ball get outside of him.

In meeting the blockers, the defensive end and the corner man (if he comes up), should always keep the ball about 1½ to 2 yards deeper than himself. The end that comes across as deep as the ball is easily turned out. The ball carrier can break inside the end and turn out again with very little, if any, loss of speed. If the ball carrier does this, the end

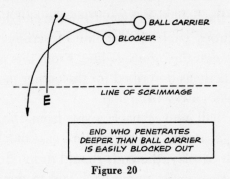

Figure 20

will have failed to contain the ball. On the other hand, if the end will always meet the blockers at a position about 1½ yards closer to the line of scrimmage than the ball itself, it will be difficult for the ball carrier to break inside without making a radical adjustment in course. By meeting the blockers in this position, the end will be able to give ground to the outside and maintain leverage on the ball, keeping it always inside.

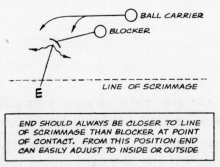

Figure 21

75

Play of the Containing Portion

When the ball starts away from the end, he immediately drops back off the line of scrimmage and looks through the offensive line. From this point, he reacts exactly as described for the corner man when the ball goes away from him.

If the ball moves back away from the line of scrimmage, as usually happens in a case of a forward pass or draw play, the ends should drop off the line of scrimmage on an angle back and to the outside. Again he is applying his maxim of "ball go, I go." Having dropped back and out he will cover the flat zone if a pass develops and react to the ball in the normal manner should the play develop into a run.

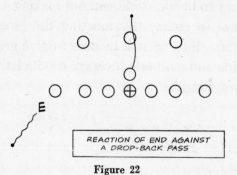

REACTION OF END AGAINST
A DROP-BACK PASS

Figure 22

PLAY OF THE WIDE SAFETY MEN—FIVE-SPOKE DEFENSE

The wide safety men of the five-spoke defense line up approximately 2½ to 3 yards outside their offensive end. (These men will vary this position slightly depending on the lateral field position of the ball as will be discussed in the chapter on pass defense.) The wide safety men look through the uncovered lineman to the ball itself. If the ball starts toward them and the linemen do not come downfield, they move absolutely laterally with the ball. They maintain this lateral movement until they are *sure* whether the play will be a run or a pass.

If the play develops into a run, they come up immediately, supporting the end, and keeping the ball inside of them.

If the play develops into a pass, they continue their lateral movement and do not come up at all to cover the flat until the middle safety man calls "clear." This is a most important assignment. The wide safety must never assume that the middle man has moved over. The wide safety's assignment is always to be deep enough and wide enough to cover any pass thrown to his side of the field. If he drops back and out against passes, no touchdowns will be completed over him. On the other hand, if he assumes that on the running fake the middle safety has moved over to cover behind him and therefore he comes up to cover the flat, a touchdown will result if the middle safety is slow or out of position. The wide safety man must never come up on a running pass toward him unless he has heard the call "clear" from the middle safety.

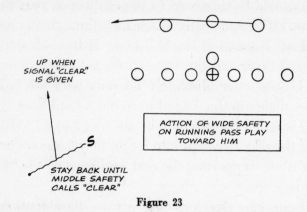

Figure 23

Many coaches will disagree with this type of defensive play on the part of the wide safety. It is true that most running passes will be covered better in the flat zone if the wide safety is allowed to come up after the ball has moved 4 to 5 yards laterally. However, the flat pass seldom, if ever, results in a breakaway touchdown. If the wide safety comes up and the ball is thrown behind him, a touchdown almost inevitably results. It seems best to have the wide safety cover deep until the middle safety is sure that he has moved over far enough to cover the deep outside zone against a running pass.

If the ball moves away from the wide safety, he should move reasonably fast on an angle back and towards the ball. As he makes this movement, he again keys the movement of the uncovered lineman to determine whether it is a pass or a run. *Until he is sure the play is a run, he should continue to move back as he moves across the field.*

PLAY OF THE MIDDLE SAFETY MAN—FIVE-SPOKE DEFENSE

The middle safety should line up 10 to 12 yards deep directly in front of the ball. He, too, should key an uncovered lineman. The key for the middle safety will be either the center or the guards.

The middle safety reacts to the ball exactly as do the other men in the containing portion of the defense. If the ball moves quickly to either side, the middle safety, with a shuffling step, should start moving with the ball, giving ground slightly back. The farther the ball moves in a lateral direction, the

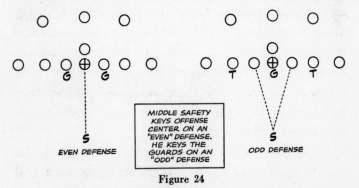

EVEN DEFENSE

MIDDLE SAFETY KEYS OFFENSE CENTER ON AN "EVEN" DEFENSE. HE KEYS THE GUARDS ON AN "ODD" DEFENSE

ODD DEFENSE

Figure 24

79

faster the middle safety will move and at the same time continue to deepen his angle backward. As he makes this adjustment, he will key the uncovered lineman. If a movement on the part of the lineman indicates that the play is a run, he will stop dropping back and will come up quickly to support the play. If the ball does not move in either lateral direction but moves back towards the offensive team's goal line, as occurs on a drop back pass play, the middle safety should drop straight back to cover the deep middle zone.

ADJUSTMENTS TO FLANKERS— FIVE-SPOKE DEFENSE

The five-spoke defense adjusts very easily to flankers. The rules for these adjustments are:

Ends: (1) If your end is a flanker, drop back and outside, into a position shallow enough so that the end cannot cross in front of you to catch a quick

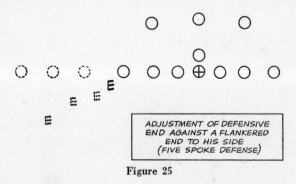

ADJUSTMENT OF DEFENSIVE
END AGAINST A FLANKERED
END TO HIS SIDE
(FIVE SPOKE DEFENSE)

Figure 25

pass. The lateral width of the flankered end from his tackle will determine the exact position of the defensive end. If the end is flankered 5 yards, a defensive end should be approximately 2 yards off the line of scrimmage and 2½ to 3 yards inside of the offensive end. If the offensive end is flankered 10 yards from the tackle, the defensive end should be approximately 4 yards behind the line of scrimmage and 5 yards inside of the defensive end. By taking this position, the defensive end puts himself between the end and the passer and thereby makes it difficult for the offense to complete a quick pass. (2) The end makes no other adjustments to any type of flanker. He lines up and continues to play his regular defensive position, reacting to the ball exactly as he would if it were a balanced formation and no flanker were out. (3) The wide safety man has only one assignment. If any opponent flankers to his side,

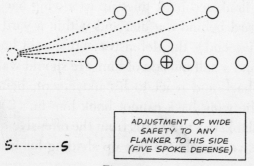

ADJUSTMENT OF WIDE
SAFETY TO ANY
FLANKER TO HIS SIDE
(FIVE SPOKE DEFENSE)

Figure 26

he must put himself in position to cover the flanker in the deep outside zone regardless of whom he may be. In other words, if either end, the on halfback, the fullback, or the opposite halfback are lined up as a flanker to his side, he must widen and be in position to drop back and cover the deep outside. (4) The middle safety has no flanker adjustment other than to favor slightly, before the ball is snapped, the side of the flanker if the flanker is set to the wide field.

The only difficult adjustment to flankers from the five-spoke defense is teaching the ends to drop off and play properly against the flankered end. The end must also be aware of the lateral position of a flankered back who is out to his side. He makes no adjustment of assignment regardless of whether it is the on halfback, fullback, or the crossed halfback. But he should take his position in relation to the flankered back according to the following rules: (1) If the flankered back lines up as a wing back (that is, a yard behind the line and within a yard of the offensive end), the defensive end should line up a yard and a half outside of him. He should watch the wing back and react to his movement, being sure that the wing back cannot hook him in. (2) If the back flankers 3 to 5 yards from the offensive end, the defensive end should line up shading his inside. As the ball is snapped, he should charge the flankered back, hit him, play him one hundred percent, and force him to the outside. It is possible the end playing in this manner may be blocked by the back, but the time element involved in moving the ball to this wide area gives the end time to recover from the

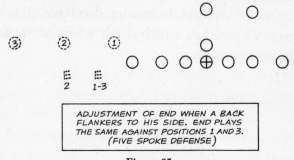

ADJUSTMENT OF END WHEN A BACK FLANKERS TO HIS SIDE. END PLAYS THE SAME AGAINST POSITIONS 1 AND 3. (FIVE SPOKE DEFENSE)

Figure 27

block, get back on his feet, and handle the play normally. (3) If the flankered back is further than 5 yards from the end, the defensive end lines up normally and plays his regular assignment exactly as he would when no back is flankered.

This description of the play of the four-spoke and five-spoke containing unit of the defensive team is an attempt to list the basic rules of movement for these units of defense. It is totally an explanation of theory against a balanced formation together with basic adjustments to flankers. In actual competition lateral field position of the ball determines, to a tremendous degree, the actual alignment and movement of these men. This phase of the defense will be discussed in detail in the chapter on pass defense. However, it is well that the reader understand thoroughly the basic theory of play of these units. The explanation is an attempt to make the theory absolutely clear without becoming involved in minor changes of position, which result when lateral field position is considered.

7

Play of the Forcing Unit of the Defense

By applying simple mathematics, it is easily seen that when a four man containing unit is used by the defensive team, seven men remain to play the forcing unit. In a like manner, if five men comprise the containing unit of defense, only six remain to force the issue.

There are several basic alignments for the forcing part of the defense when the four-spoke containing unit is used. The most normal defenses are:

1. A seven-box defense.
2. A five-four defense.
3. A six-three defense.
4. A four-five defense.

All of these defenses may be played in a variety of ways, but the essentials of the containing portion remain exactly the same. Four men are involved in it; they have one unvarying assignment. The forcing portion may be played in a wide variety of ways from each of the alignments given above.

The five-spoke containing unit leaves six men in the forcing portion of the defense. The standard alignments used from a five-spoke containing unit are:

1. Six-two defense.
2. Five-three defense.
3. Seven-one defense.

Again a great number of variations can be used from each of the defenses listed. It should be remembered, however, that when a five-spoke containing unit is used there is one less man in the forcing unit. Consequently, the five-spoke unit will probably *contain* the offensive team better but will *not force* nearly so well. Conversely, the four-spoke unit has seven men to force the issue. The four-spoke group will probably not only *contain* the offense quite so well, but the seven men forcing will do a more adequate job of making a real issue at the line of scrimmage with the offensive team.

From the different alignments given above, many *defensive stunts* may be used. A defensive stunt is an unusual maneuver or charge on the part of the defensive player.

Normally, when the ball is snapped, defensive linemen will charge over the man they face. In like

manner, defensive linebackers will react normally
to their key and the movement of the ball. A "stunt"
on the part of the lineman would be a radical movement to his left or to his right away from the man
he would normally charge. A stunt on the part of
the linebacker would be to charge as a lineman
either straight ahead or through the gap to his left
or to his right.

Stunts can be very effective against a poorly
drilled offensive team. They have a great deal of
value in that if successful, they will quickly force
the issue with the offensive team. If by stunting the
defensive linemen are able to penetrate quickly into
the backfield because the offensive men have missed
their assignment, stunts are most worthwhile. However, if the stunt is not successful, the defensive men
may have moved themselves out of position. In this
case they are never in quite as good a position to
control their territory and pursue the ball, since their
stunt has started them at an angle which is not in
the proper direction in relation to the play being run.
They must stop, regain their balance, and then make
a radical adjustment back into their angle of pursuit.

This brings up a very pertinent question. When
should the defense stunt?

Normally speaking, if the defense is physically as
capable as the offensive team, stunting should not

be necessary nor should it be considered a sound defensive practice. If the defense does not stunt and the containing portion functions properly, the angle of pursuit should stop all long runs and quickly support against all short passes.

When stunts are used, even though the containing portion functions properly, the forcing portion of the defense, because of their stunts, may be unable to recover quickly enough to adjust to their angle of pursuit. This failure may cause a lack of quick support to the containing unit and long runs may develop. It seems logical, therefore, to assume that it is sound practice to stunt the defense only when normal defensive charges are not capable of stopping the offensive team. However, if a normal defense is able to contain the offense and to hold them to short gains, stunts are seldom advisable. The offensive team will usually make an error if they must put the ball into play a great number of times before they score.

8

Proper Utilization of Personnel

One of the most difficult, most important problems confronting the coach is the placement of individual players in particular defensive positions to best utilize the player's natural ability. There are many factors to be considered here. The most important one is the limitation of practice time. In present day college football practice time has been drastically limited by the rules of the National Collegiate Athletic Association and the various conferences. There is no longer enough practice time for the coach to teach a football player as much as he would like to. The same situation prevails in most high schools. Because of this time limitation, it follows that the limited hours available will be utilized to better advantage if each individual has very few fundamentals to master.

89

Proper Utilization of Personnel

The defensive personnel should be organized in such a manner that the same fundamentals for most men on the team can be adapted to a wide variety of defensive alignments.

This objective can be realized by organizing the defensive team into units as was described previously. There are four categories of personnel within the defensive alignment: (1) defensive linemen, (2) defensive ends, (3) defensive linebackers, and (4) defensive secondary men.

In changing the defense from a 5-4-2 defense to a 6-2-2-1 (going from a four-spoke to a five-spoke defense) ten players have the same position and type of assignment. However, one defensive end does not. This man must function as a secondary man when the four-spoke containing unit is used, and as an end when the five-spoke pattern is employed.

With the exception of this man, none of the other members of the defensive team, in order to go from one alignment to the other, ever need to adjust or learn to play any other basic defensive fundamentals. One end continues to play end. The guards and tackles remain linemen at all times. The center and the fullback continue to be linebackers. The quarterback and halfbacks remain as secondary men all of the time. Only one end needs to know how to play two positions.

Proper Utilization of Personnel

In setting up the defensive team, we believe it is best to teach the left end to play the corner man in the four-spoke defense. The left end becomes a secondary man when the four-spoke is employed, and plays an end when the five-spoke containing unit is used. You will recall that his reaction as a defensive end in the five-spoke defense is practically the same as his reaction as the corner man in the four-spoke defense. The only real difference is that he meets the blockers a little bit quicker on plays to his side when playing as an end.

It is sound also to teach the right end to play as a defensive lineman as well as an end. When the four-spoke pattern is employed, the right end on certain defenses will play as a defensive lineman and on others as an end. With this fundamental added, each end has two defensive positions to learn and to master. The left end must play as a secondary man and as an end. The right end should be able to play as an end and as a lineman.

With this type of organization, a variety of alignments can be used without confusion by the defensive team. Adjustments from one defensive set-up to another cause no particular problem because the fundamental execution at the snap of the ball on the part of nine men of the defensive team remains the same. If they can execute their basic fundamental assignment, they can play from any alignment. Only two men need to know two sets of fundamentals.

We believe very strongly that this type of defensive organization pays great dividends. If a man is a linebacker on one defense, a lineman on another defense, and an end on another defense, he probably will not be able to master all of the fundamentals equally well, and unquestionably he will not be as proficient at all three as he could be at one. If the fundamentals for each man remain the same regardless of the alignment used, he can play all defenses equally well since all he must learn is where to line up. He knows by habit how to execute the fundamentals of his position as soon as the ball is snapped.

Other plans similar in theory but different in the placement of personnel can be used as effectively as the one outlined above. For example, the fullback may be played as a corner man in a four-spoke set-up and as a linebacker in a five-spoke set-up. The organizational theory remains the same. However, we believe each defensive coach should build his team within the four categories listed. Every effort should be made to reduce to the absolute minimum the number of men who must adjust from one position to the other as the alignment changes.

9

Defense 72

Defense 72 is the basic defense played at the University of Oklahoma and has been our best over-all defense for the past several years. And while, like all defenses, it has a few inherent weaknesses, it is very sound against the basic "T" formation.

This is a four-spoke defense. Seven men comprise the forcing unit of the defense. The assignments for the individual players are as follows:

Left tackle and right end: Line up almost in front of the offensive end. As the ball is snapped, charge hard, straight into the end, being sure that the end is not able to *block you in*. React to and key the end. (1) If the end blocks to the inside, do *not* penetrate, but move along the line of scrimmage with him, closing the gap to your inside. (2) If the end attempts to block you out, fight the pressure. Hold your ground as well as possible. Do not be faked to the inside where the end will be able to reverse body

Defense 72

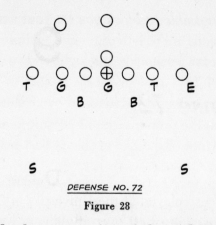

DEFENSE NO. 72

Figure 28

block and take you in. (3) If the end attempts to take you in by "hook" blocking, give ground quickly along the scrimmage to the outside. *Remember your basic assignment. The end must never block you in.* (4) If the end attempts to get downfield, hit him and hold him up as long as you can. Never let him cross the line of scrimmage quickly or easily. (5) When the end does get away from you and the ball has started in the opposite direction, *you are the leverage man.* Before chasing the ball, penetrate across the line of scrimmage until you are *as deep as the ball.* Then turn and chase the play as rapidly as possible.

Left guard and right tackle: Line up almost head up with the offensive tackle. As the ball is snapped, charge straight into the tackle being sure that the tackle is *not able to block you in.* Your assignments and reactions are exactly the same as those given for the defensive left tackle and right end, with the exception of (5). If your tackle is able to get away from you and move downfield, you should move quickly on the proper angle of pursuit in an attempt to get in front of the ball at the earliest possible moment.

Right guard: Line up head up with the offensive center about 2 to 2½ feet off the line of scrimmage. Vary the strength of your charge from play to play. Occasionally, charge hard into the center and attempt to knock him back. Most of the time, charge with just enough force to control the offensive center. Basically, *you must never allow the center to cut you either way.* You must control both sides of the center, maintaining your ability to move to either side. If you charge hard, you can be cut to one side more easily by the center. If you take a soft, controlled charge, it will be difficult for the center to take you either way. But if you charge too softly, the center will be able to knock you back. In about one out of four or five plays, charge hard and attempt to knock the center straight back. The rest of the time play a "controlled" game. This variance in the strength of your charge will make it more difficult for the center to block you as he cannot anticipate the charge you will use.

Since he must control both sides of one offensive man, the right guard has the most difficult defensive assignment on this defense. This is a very difficult thing to do against an equally capable opponent. All other linemen need protect only one side to have the defense hold up adequately.

Linebackers: Line up a yard and a half off the line of scrimmage on the outside shoulder of the offensive guard. React and key the movement of the guard. (1) If the guard drives out on you, charge straight into the guard. Contact him on his outside shoulder. Be positive that the guard is not able *to block you in.* (2) If the guard blocks aggressively to his left or to his right, shoot the gap. As you cross the line of scrimmage, stay as close to the power block made by the guard as is possible. By so doing you will be hard to trap. For example, when the guard blocks in on the man over the center, the opposite guard may pull to trap block. If the linebacker shoots at the spot where the offensive guard was lined up, a big gap will open up between himself and the man on the center, making it easy for the trapping man to execute his block properly. If, on the other hand, the linebacker shoots to the inside of his "key guard" and stays as close as possible to the power block, there will be very little lateral distance between the linebacker and the defensive man on the center. The trapping man will find it very difficult to make a satisfactory block. (3) If the guard pulls in either direction, move with the guard, find the ball, and pursue on the proper angle. (4) If the guard straightens up and drops back to make a pass-protection block, move quickly to the hook zone and play the ball.

Corner men (left end and right halfback): Line up 3 yards behind the line of scrimmage and 4 to 5 yards outside the offensive end. If the ball starts towards you, give ground laterally to the outside with the ball as you exercise your key of watching the uncovered offensive lineman. If the lineman crosses the line of scrimmage to come downfield, move up immediately and force the play while maintaining outside position on the ball. Remember to meet the blocker so that the ball is at least 1½ to 2 yards deeper behind the line of scrimmage than you are. From this position you will be able to give ground back and to the outside to keep the ball from getting around you. Always avoid coming up so fast that you overrun the ball, that is, get deeper than the ball itself. If you do this, you will be blocked out easily, and the ball carrier will move on the same course with no reduction in speed. He will go inside of you, and yet be outside of the rest of the team exactly as

97

he would if you were too shallow and were blocked in. When the lineman crosses the line of scrimmage and you react, you must attempt to close to the inside in order to narrow the lateral distance between yourself and the outside lineman. If no linemen are downfield and the ball continues laterally past the position occupied by the offensive tackle, you should begin to give ground back and to the outside. Continue on this course until you are sure the play is a run. Only two things will determine this: (1) A lineman comes downfield, or the ball itself crosses the line of scrimmage. If the ball stops moving laterally and no linemen are downfield, you should discontinue your lateral movement and drop straight back to become a pass defender. (2) If the ball goes away from you, drop straight back quickly and key to see whether you should continue straight back as a pass defender or move across the field as you would do in the case of a running play. If the ball moves back away from the line of scrimmage, drop back and out, playing pass until you are positive the play is a run.

Middle safeties: Line up 8 to 9 yards deep on the inside shoulder of the offensive end. As the ball is snapped, move with it and react to your key, the offensive guard. (1) If the guard is downfield, come up quickly to support for a running play. (2) If the guard is not downfield, continue to move with the ball. The farther the ball moves laterally, the farther you should move in that direction, at the same time giving ground back. Continue to move back playing pass-defense until you are positive it is a run. Remember you are only *sure* it is a running play if the ball or a lineman (ineligible receiver) crosses the line of scrimmage.

From this defensive alignment several stunts may be used. The basic stunts are cross charges by the linebacker with the linemen in front of him. Two of these work reasonably well.

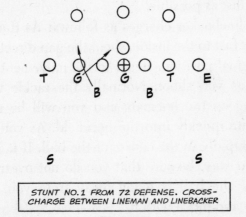

STUNT NO.1 FROM 72 DEFENSE. CROSS-CHARGE BETWEEN LINEMAN AND LINEBACKER

Figure 29

(1) On the first stunt, the tackle charges hard to the inside, while the linebacker shoots the gap over the position where his tackle originally lined up. In

executing this cross charge, the assignment of the lineman is as follows: Line up exactly as you would on regular Defense 72. As the ball is snapped, charge hard at the juncture of the neck and shoulder of the offensive guard. Play the guard's head. If the guard blocks *out* on you, flatten your course, staying close to the line of scrimmage so that the guard cannot block you out. If you watch his head carefully enough you will be able to adjust your course quickly so that the guard will have trouble getting in position to block you out. If the guard does not turn out on you, penetrate on the original angle and get to the ball as fast as possible.

The linebacker charges as follows: As the guard charges fast to the inside, shoot the gap directly over his original position. React to the movement of the tackle as you shoot. Normally the tackle will be blocking on the lineman, and you will be able to penetrate quickly into the backfield. As you shoot, adjust rapidly to the course of the ball. If it is coming your way, be sure that you do not overrun the play. If the ball is going away from you, adjust quickly and move with it.

The second stunt has both the tackle and linebacker shooting through the gap to their outside. This defensive charge is most effective if it is used when a wide play is called. It is executed as follows:

Tackle: Line up exactly as you would for regular Defense 72. As the ball is snapped, shoot fast to the outside of the offensive tackle, attempting to get

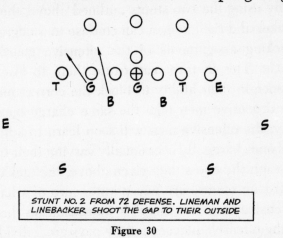

STUNT NO. 2 FROM 72 DEFENSE. LINEMAN AND LINEBACKER SHOOT THE GAP TO THEIR OUTSIDE

Figure 30

penetration through the gap between the offensive end and tackle. Be sure the tackle does not block you in. Having penetrated, react quickly to the ball.

Linebacker: Line up exactly as you would for Defense 72. As the ball is snapped, shoot the gap fast between the offensive tackle and the offensive guard. React quickly to the ball.

When this charge is used, the man playing over the center, the right guard, should protect to the side of the cross charge so that he will be in position to stop the play if the ball should be run between the offensive center and the offensive guard. There is no linebacker in position to support this hole when the linebacker shoots. Therefore, it is necessary for the middle guard to lend some support to this area.

By using the two stunts outlined above, the linebacker and the lineman can confuse to a degree the blocking assignments of the offensive guard and tackle. This in turn may cause them to lose confidence in their ability to block the correct man. If the defensive men take the same charge on every play, the offensive men will soon learn to adjust to this one charge. By occasionally varying their tactics through the two stunts given above, the tackle and guard on offense are never quite sure of what the defensive men will do. This indecision on the part of the offensive players usually pays great dividends to the defense.

Another type of stunt which is very effective from this defensive alignment is to slant the entire five linemen to one side or the other. These stunts may be called by simply adding the words "slant left" or "slant right" to the defense. For example, "72, slant left" would be played as follows: All linemen take their position exactly as they would for Defense 72, except that they should drop back off the line of scrimmage approximately a foot to 18 inches. As the ball moves, all men move very quickly to their left. The left tackle should step fast *outside* of the offensive end, and, having gained this new position, react to the ball by playing exactly as he would for Defense 72. The left guard will shoot the gap between the offensive end and tackle. The guard over the

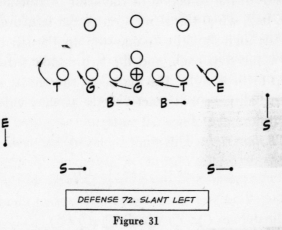

DEFENSE 72. SLANT LEFT

Figure 31

center will charge at the face of the offensive guard to his left being sure that the guard does not block him in. The right tackle should charge hard at the face of the offensive guard to his left, being sure that this guard does not block him out. He will adjust his course by watching the head of the guard exactly as he would in making the first cross charge stunt, described above. The right end charges hard to his left through the gap between the end and the tackle. As the linemen are moving to the left, the two linebackers take one step to their right, and key their guards just as they do on regular Defense 72. It is also well to have the containing portion of the defense take one step anticipating that the ball may move opposite to the direction of the slant. At the snap of the ball, when the slant is on to the left, the right corner man should take one step up, the left corner man one step back, and the two middle safeties a step to their right. Having taken this initial movement, all men will react exactly as they would in their normal Defense 72 pattern.

72 slant right. This stunt is played exactly as "slant

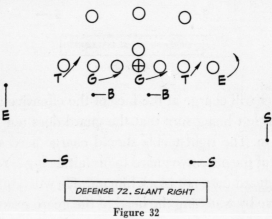

DEFENSE 72. SLANT RIGHT

Figure 32

left," except that the linemen move to their right while the linebackers and containing men cover to the left.

There is one other stunt used with this defense

that is quite effective, particularly in rushing the passer. This stunt involves the middle guard and the linebackers. The middle guard slants hard to one side or the other. If the middle guard is slanting to

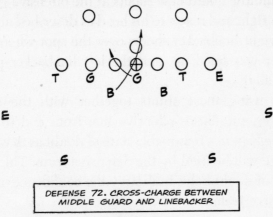

DEFENSE 72. CROSS-CHARGE BETWEEN
MIDDLE GUARD AND LINEBACKER

Figure 33

the left, he will charge straight at the face of the offensive guard to his left. As he makes this charge, he should watch the head of the offensive guard, making sure that the guard is never able to block him in. If the guard is coming at him, he must flatten his course and work to the outside around the guard's head. While the middle guard is charging in this manner, the left linebacker must shoot the gap very quickly over the spot where the center was lined up. As he makes this charge, he should react to the block of the center and then pursue the ball accurately.

105

The right linebacker plays his normal assignment when this stunt is on.

The same variation can be used in exactly the same way by the middle guard and the right linebacker. The middle guard now shoots at the offensive guard to his right and reacts to his head as described above. The right linebacker shoots over the spot where the center was lined up, and the left linebacker plays normally.

By using these stunts together with the cross charges, the entire offensive line from end to end can be kept in a reasonable state of doubt as to which charge will be used by the defensive team. This element of doubt helps to destroy the confidence of the offensive team.

10

Defense 54

Defense 54 is in many ways similar to Defense 72. Basically it is stronger against a forward pass game than Defense 72. On the other hand, it is not quite as effective against a running attack as is Defense 72. Defense 54 is played in the following manner:

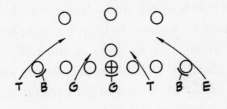

DEFENSE NO. 54

Figure 34

Left tackle and right end: Line up about 1½ yards outside of the offensive end facing slightly to the inside so that the hip of the offensive end is on a line between you and the fullback. As the ball is snapped, charge hard straight along this course through the hip of the end, penetrating towards the fullback. If the offensive end charges forward, you will not contact his hips as he will have moved ahead out of the way. However, if the end does not move forward quickly, your shoulder will hit the hip of the end, and knock him off balance.

As you continue to penetrate on this course to the inside, watch the blocking develop. If the ball is *coming towards you*, penetrate until you meet the blocker. Hit the blocker hard enough to knock him back. Then try to recover to the outside.

If the ball is going away from you, deepen and put yourself in position to keep leverage on the ball. As soon as you are as deep as the ball, chase the play. Remember, when the ball moves away from you it is vitally important to get depth quickly.

If a drop back pass develops, continue rushing on a course towards the fullback, fight through the blockers to the passer but maintain leverage on the ball. Be positive that you are not blocked in by a pass-protection blocker so that the passer can run around you to the outside. You must *keep leverage on the ball* on *all drop tackle passes* and on all plays when the ball goes away from you.

Left guard and left tackle: Line up on the inside shoulder of the offensive tackle facing slightly to the inside. As the ball is snapped, charge hard at the juncture of the head and shoulder of the offensive guard. As you make this charge, watch the head of the offensive guard. You must never allow his head to get inside of you so that you can be *driven out.* Your only responsibility on this defense is to close the gap between yourself and the middle guard. If the offensive guard charges forward, continue on your normal course. If he pulls to either side, continue on your normal course. If he blocks out on you, flatten your charge immediately and be sure that he does not block you out.

Right guard: Line up head up with the offensive center, charge hard into the center about one out of four times. The other three times take the controlled charge. Be sure that the center cannot cut you either way. (The right guard's defensive assignment on Defense 54 is exactly the same as it is on Defense 72.)

Linebackers: Line up in either an upright or three-point stance 18 inches behind the line of scrimmage. Face the inside shoulder of the offensive end. As the ball is snapped, charge hard at the inside shoulder of the offensive end. Hit the end. Never let the end get off the line of scrimmage to *your inside.* If the end is blocking in on you, fight through him and maintain your ability to move. Recover on your angle of pursuit. If the end is trying to go downfield, hit him and hold him up as long as possible. Then recover with your normal angle of pursuit.

Note: The linebacker and the right end on the right side (linebacker and left tackle on the left side) should work as a double team to hold up and delay the offensive end. In order to do this it is of paramount importance that they both take their positions absolutely accurately. If their positions are taken exactly as described above, the offensive end will always be hit on the line of scrimmage, since one of the two defensive men always has position on him and both of them are driving at him with the snap of the ball. If the end moves straight ahead, he will be hit and knocked to the outside by the linebacker. If the end fails to charge forward or moves to his outside, he will be hit hard by the end. If these two men, the linebacker and the end, take their positions accurately it is virtually impossible for the offensive player to get downfield quickly. When the end cannot get downfield quickly, the threat of the long forward pass is reduced.

Since almost all of the forcing portion of the defense is on the line of scrimmage in this alignment, there are not many stunts that can be used effectively. However, since this is basically a pass defense, a seven-man rush by both linebackers with the five linemen is, at times, most effective. When the rush is called, it is executed in the following manner: The left tackle and right end line up exactly as they do

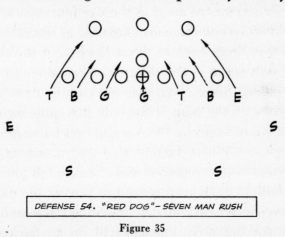

DEFENSE 54. "RED DOG"—SEVEN MAN RUSH

Figure 35

for regular Defense 54. However, their angle of charge will be wider. Instead of driving at the full-back, they drive straight at the offensive halfback on their side. While driving at this angle, both men re-act to the ball exactly as described above.

The left guard and right tackle play regular Defense 54 as described above. The right guard executes regular Defense 54 as described above.

The linebackers take their positions exactly as they do on regular Defense 54. However, with the snap of the ball, both men charge hard through the gap between the offensive end and tackle, and then react to the ball.

This seems like a very simple stunt but it is most effective against a team that throws a great many passes and uses as many as three or four men as pass receivers. When three men are used as receivers and one man drops back to throw the ball, it is obvious that only seven of the eleven men remain to protect the passer. Since seven men are rushing from good angles with the snap of the ball, it is quite easy for one man to avoid his blocker and "get home free" to the passer. When the offensive team has four men assigned as pass receivers and one man left to throw the ball, only six men remain to protect the passer. If seven men rush with determination it is most likely that one defensive lineman will get to the passer before he is able to throw the ball.

If you compare Defense 54 with Defense 72, you will see that the assignments are virtually the same. The containing portion of the defense plays exactly alike in both instances. The left tackle and right end have almost similar assignments.

The left guard and right tackle line up in a slightly different position, but the charge they take is exactly the same as the charge used for the inside cross charge as described in the stunts for Defense 72.

The right guard, too, executes the same assignment on both defenses.

The linebackers do have a different assignment. When playing Defense 72, they react to the movement of the offensive guard. On Defense 54 they play exclusively against the offensive end. These are two different assignments.

Thus, in comparing the two defenses, you can see that only the linebackers actually have anything radically different to do as the alignment is changed from one defense to the other. Yet the two defenses present an entirely different problem to the offensive team.

In straight-away Defense 72, together with the stunts, you have a very strong running defense. In Defense 54 you have a very strong pass defense coupled with an excellent pass rush when the linebackers shoot. These two defenses, played as a combination on alternate downs, give excellent variety to the defensive pattern and create a real problem of adjustment for the offensive team. Yet very little change in assignments is required by anyone making up the defensive eleven. The two plans co-ordinate very well together.

11

Defense 45

Defense 45 is the last of the four-man containing unit defenses to consider. It has many of the same assignments as one of the five-man containing unit defenses, which will be described later, but it is played within the framework of the four-man containing unit. Actually, the linemen and the linebackers react almost identically as they do for Defense 60. The assignments are as follows:

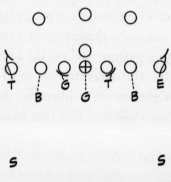

DEFENSE NO. 45

Figure 36

Left tackle and right end: Line up 18 inches off the line of scrimmage on the inside shoulder of the offensive end. As the ball is snapped, charge hard at the head of the offensive end. Hit the end. *Be sure the end does not block you in.* Hold him on the line of scrimmage as long as possible. Work to his outside. Then react to the ball.

If the ball is coming your way, try to maintain outside position, giving ground along the line of scrimmage so that the ball will not get outside of you. If the ball is moving away from you, deepen quickly until you are as deep as the ball. At this point, turn and follow the play. You are the leverage man on this defense. If a drop-back pass develops, rush the passer as hard as possible but be sure that you maintain outside leverage and are not taken in by a pass-protection blocker.

Left guard and right tackle: Line up head up with the offensive guards about 2 feet behind the line of scrimmage. As the ball is snapped, charge hard straight into the offensive guards, controlling them. Never let the guards *block you in.* React to the blocks of the guard in front of you, the center, and the tackle to your outside, keying rapidly on their movements as you take your charge. As you control the guard, react quickly to the ball and recover on the proper angle of pursuit.

Linebackers: Line up a yard and a half behind the line of scrimmage on the outside shoulder of the offensive tackle. Watch the tackle and key him exactly as you do the guard on Defense 72. (1) If the tackle drives out at you, charge straight into him. Control him. Attempt to drive him back. *Be sure he does not block you in.* (2) If the tackle blocks aggressively to either side, shoot the gap quickly. Be sure that you are close to the side of the power, double-team block so that you will not be vulnerable to a trap. (3) If the tackle pulls in either direction, move with him. (4) If the tackle drops back to make a pass-protection block, drop quickly to the hook zone and play the ball.

Right guard: Line up head up with the offensive center 2 yards behind the line of scrimmage. Look through the center to the quarterback. Key both men. (1) If the center blocks aggressively to either side and the ball moves *away from* the center's block, maintain your position until you are sure the ball will not come back between your guards. When you are *sure* the ball has moved out of the area, move toward the ball carrier, being positive to stay *behind* the ball so that you do not overrun it and can fill from the inside angle. (2) If the center drives out at you, move in quickly and hit him. Do not let him cut you either way. React to the ball. (3) If the cen-

ter makes a pass-protection block, drop back quickly
and play pass defense.

The four men in the containing portion of the defense play their regular assignments as described for
the other defenses of this type.

There are a number of possible stunts from this
alignment. The stunts usually can be played by three
distinct groups. The left tackle and the left linebacker comprise one group. The right tackle and the
right linebacker comprise a second group, and the
two guards and the middle linebacker comprise the
third group. These three groups can set up to execute
the following stunts:

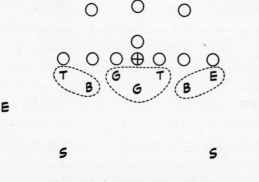

THREE STUNT GROUPS FOR DEFENSE 45

Figure 37

The tackle and the linebacker can cross charge in
either direction. For example, the tackle can drive
fast and hard to his inside, shooting the gap and

117

penetrating over the hip of the offensive tackle. As he makes this move, the linebacker charges fast to the outside, hits the end, works around him and takes over the normal assignment of the defensive tackle.

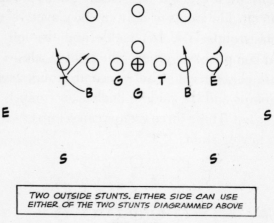

TWO OUTSIDE STUNTS. EITHER SIDE CAN USE EITHER OF THE TWO STUNTS DIAGRAMMED ABOVE

Figure 38

This cross charge may also be played by having the two men trade assignments. When this stunt is used, the tackle will execute his normal assignment and the linebacker will shoot the gap over the outside shoulder of the offensive tackle.

While using either of these stunts the linebacker must watch his key, the tackle, as he charges. If the movement of the tackle indicates that he is stunting in the wrong direction, he should immediately stop

stunting and react normally to the movement of the
offensive tackle.

As the tackles and linebackers are stunting as described, the three middle men have three possible
variations that they may use.

Stunt No. 1. The left guard and right tackle charge
to the outside past the head of the offensive guard
penetrating through the gap between the offensive
guard and the offensive tackle. As soon as they have
gained penetration, they regain their balance and

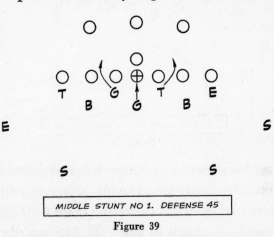

MIDDLE STUNT NO 1. DEFENSE 45

Figure 39

face up the field. They must not continue on the outside angle of charge, but must react straight ahead
so that they can adjust laterally in either direction to
pursue the ball. While the guards are taking this outside charge, the middle guard lined up on the center

will charge straight over the center, reacting to the center's blocker as he penetrates.

Stunt No. 2. Both guards slant to their left and shoot between the lineman on that side. The left guard will get his penetration between the offensive tackle and the offensive guard, while the right tackle

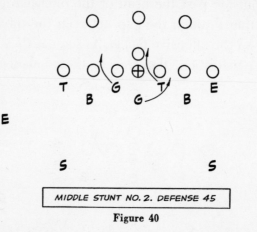

MIDDLE STUNT NO. 2. DEFENSE 45

Figure 40

will get his penetration between the offensive guard and the offensive center. Having penetrated through the gap, both men should again regain their balance and react in pursuit of the ball. The middle linebacker in this instance will step quickly to his right and charge the outside shoulder of the offensive guard. In making this play, he will fill for his tackle, who has slanted to the left.

Stunt No. 3. Both the left guard and the right

tackle charge to their right. The right tackle shoots the gap between the offensive guard and tackle, and the left guard shoots the gap between the offensive guard and the center. As they penetrate, they regain their balance and react normally to the ball. The mid-

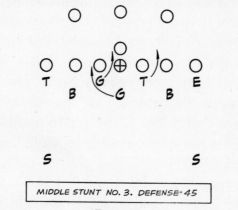

MIDDLE STUNT NO. 3. DEFENSE·45

Figure 41

dle linebacker shoots the gap to the outside shoulder of the offensive guard to his left, replacing the normal assignment of his left guard who will have angled through to the right.

These stunts in the three areas may be called independently. It does not matter, for example, whether the tackles and linebackers are stunting or playing straightaway, since any of the stunts cover the gaps along the line of scrimmage between the offensive end and tackle exactly the same as they would do if no stunt were used. Similarly, the three middle men may use any of their three stunts since each play covers all the gaps in their area. Since this defense can employ the normal charge plus two variations on the outside, and the regular charge plus three variations on the inside, the mathematical possibilities of different types of charges considered for the team as a whole are numerous. For example, if we call the cross charges on the left side "cross charge No. 1" and "cross charge No. 2," and identify the stunts on the right side as "cross charge No. 3" and "cross charge No. 4," we get 16 possible variations of defense on the outside by using these combinations.

For example, 1 and 2; 1 and 3; 1 and 4; 2 and 3; 2 and 1; 2 and 4; and so on. If you add to these variations the three different stunts used by the inside, it is readily apparent that it is possible throughout a 60-minute game to use these stunts and seldom, if ever, have the total defense be exactly the same on any two plays.

However, it should be kept in mind that when using these stunts the pursuit of the defensive team will be somewhat handicapped. If the stunts are successful in anticipating the point of attack of the offensive team, the linemen or linebackers will probably penetrate and may hit the ball carrier behind the line of scrimmage for a loss. They may even force a fumble. (*See Illustration No. 15.*) If the stunt is not fortunate enough to be directed at the point of attack, the stunting men will be moving away from the ball. They will have to stop, recover, and then react back on their normal angle of pursuit. Consequently, they will not be capable of pursuing quite as well.

This is the problem and weakness of all stunting defenses. If the stunting man penetrates quickly at the point of attack, he will, by luck or chance, appear to be very successful. On the other hand, if the stunt moves the player away from the point of attack, his pursuit will be far less efficient and the offense may have an opportunity to break for a much longer gain.

This defense, with the stunts, is very good against most types of running plays. It is particularly good against an inside running attack. It lacks, however, basic strength against wide-running pass plays.

12

Defense 60

Defense 60 will be the first of the five-man containing unit defenses to be considered. This is a standard type of defense successfully used by many teams over a period of years. In normal football terminology, this defense

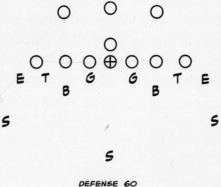

DEFENSE 60

Figure 42

is called a "wide tackle 6" or a "loose 6." The assignments for playing the defense are as follows:

Ends: Line up 2 to 3 feet outside the offensive

ends. As the ball is snapped, take one step across the line of scrimmage and play your regular key and assignment. *"Ball come, I come; ball go, I go."* This is the same reaction as was described in detail in an earlier chapter.

Tackles: Line up 18 inches off the line of scrimmage on the inside shoulder of the offensive end. React exactly as described for Defense 45.

Guards: Line up head up with the offensive guards 2 feet off the line of scrimmage. As the ball is snapped, charge hard straight into the guards being sure *that the guards are never able to block you to the outside.* React to the ball normally and pursue quickly.

Linebackers: Line up 1½ yards behind the line of scrimmage on the outside shoulder of the offensive tackle. React and key the tackle exactly as described for Defense 45. (Key the tackle exactly as you do the guard in Defense 72.)

The middle safety and wide safety men line up and play exactly as described for their movements in the five-spoke containing defense. (See Chapter 6.)

There are two stunts which work very effectively from this alignment. The stunting units, in this instance, are made up of three men each. The left tackle, left guard, and linebacker comprise one unit.

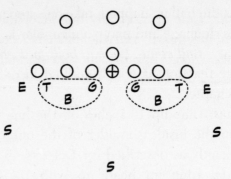

TWO STUNT UNITS OF DEFENSE 60

Figure 43

The right tackle, right guard, and linebacker make up the other unit. The stunts used by each unit are called *"60 inside"* and *"60 outside."*

ASSIGNMENTS FOR "60 INSIDE"

Tackles: Line up normally. Instead of charging into the ends, shoot the gap fast, through the hip of the offensive tackle. As you make this charge, key the tackle. If he turns out on you, flatten your charge so that he cannot block you out. Having made penetration, react normally to the ball. Remember, if the ball is going away from you, you must deepen quickly to get as far behind the line of scrimmage as the ball, and then pursue from there so that you will be able to keep leverage against any type of reverse play.

Guards: Line up normally but shoot the gap fast between the guard and the offensive center. Get penetration; react rapidly on your normal angle of pursuit.

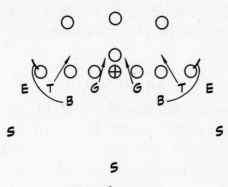

DEFENSE "60 INSIDE"
Figure 44

Linebackers: Line up normally but at the snap of the ball, charge to the outside at the offensive ends. Hit the ends, trying to knock them back and hold them up. Never let the ends *block you in.* As the ends get away from you, make them go off the line of scrimmage to your inside. Having played the end in this manner, react on your normal angle of pursuit to the ball.

Note: As the linebacker makes this stunt he must watch his normal key, the tackle. If the movement of the tackle indicates that the play is to the opposite side, the linebacker should not continue on the out-

127

side course to hit the end, but should stop and immediately react back to the opposite side. Two
movements of the tackle usually indicate that the
play is going to the other side. If the tackle pulls to
his inside, or, if he blocks out aggressively on the
offensive tackle, the play will almost always go to the
opposite side.

60 OUTSIDE

In executing this stunt the tackle plays his normal
assignment of Defense 60. The guard lines up nor-

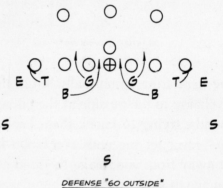

DEFENSE "60 OUTSIDE"

Figure 45

mally but shoots the gap fast to the outside, penetrating between the offensive guard and the offensive tackle. The linebacker lines up normally but
shoots the gap between the offensive guard and
center.

128

Again, while executing this stunt, the linebacker should make every effort to key his tackle normally. If the movement of the tackle shows that the play is going to the outside, the linebacker should not continue to stunt. He should stop and react back to his outside on a normal angle of pursuit.

REGULAR 60

From a containing standpoint, the Regular 60 Defense is very strong. It also provides excellent pass coverage. In studying each man's assignment carefully it will be noted that if a normal drop back pass develops, seven men will drop back to cover. These men are the two ends, both linebackers, and the three deep safety men. In addition, both tackles will be hitting and holding up the offensive ends. Against passes you have excellent coverage and have caused a reasonable delay on the part of the receivers coming downfield. As a compensating factor it must be noted that the defense does *not* rush the passer to any great degree.

Against running plays it is very effective in containing the ball, since both the linebackers and the ends react on reliable keys to pursue the ball while only the guards and tackles make a penetrating charge. With seven men free behind the line of scrimmage to pursue the play, it is reasonable to assume that the offense can make a succession of short gains, but since it is virtually impossible to block all seven moving men in the secondary, it will be most difficult for the offense to make a long breakaway touchdown run.

This defense is perhaps most effective when the offensive team is in a disadvantageous down and yardage situation. Conversely, it is a very poor short yardage defense. If the yardage, for example, is fourth down and 3 yards to gain, almost any straight ahead play can pick up the necessary 3 yards. On the other hand, if the down and yardage situation is fourth down and 10 yards to go, the seven free, moving, pursuing men can usually stop the offensive team short of the first down.

60 INSIDE AND 60 OUTSIDE

When the 60 Inside and 60 Outside stunts are added to the normal pattern of play, the forcing portion of the defense becomes a little bit tougher for the offensive team to cope with. With three possible charges on the part of the guards and tackles, together with the filling movement into the two different holes on the part of the linebackers, the possibility of the offense missing some of their blocking assignments is increased. If the offense can be maneuvered into errors in their blocking assignments, the forcing portion of the defense will be adequate, and this alignment can be used with great success.

There are two other variations of 60 Defense which can be used to change the pace, and which alter the basic assignments of the defense very little. These two plays are: Cross Charge 60 and Tight Tackle 60.

CROSS CHARGE 60

On the Cross Charge 60 Defense the ends, guards, and three safety men line up and play exactly as they do on regular Defense 60. Only the tackles and the linebackers change their alignment and their charge.

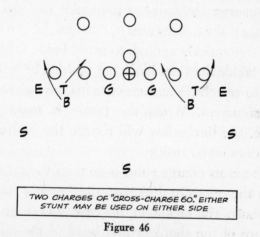

TWO CHARGES OF "CROSS-CHARGE 60." EITHER STUNT MAY BE USED ON EITHER SIDE

Figure 46

When Cross Charge 60 is used, the defensive tackle lines up exactly in the gap between the offen-

131

sive end and tackle. He plays about 18 inches off the line of scrimmage and should be facing directly up the field (not pointed to the inside). The linebacker takes his position directly behind his own tackle.

Before the ball is snapped, the two men make a decision as to who will move to which side. If the tackle is to move to the left, the linebacker will charge to the right. Conversely, if the tackle is to charge to the right, the linebacker will move to the left.

The assignments are as follows: When the tackle is moving to his right, he will dive hard at the juncture of the shoulder and neck of the offensive tackle. As he charges, he will key the tackle in order to be sure that if the tackle turns out on him, he can flatten his charge quickly enough to avoid being taken out. If the tackle does not block out on him, he will continue to penetrate and execute his normal Defense 60 assignment. When the tackle is making this charge, the linebacker will charge the end exactly as he does on 60 Inside.

If the cross charge stunt is on with the men moving in the opposite direction, they simply trade assignments. The tackle, in this case, will drive at the juncture of the shoulder and head of the offensive end, keying the end and maintaining his ability to flatten his charge to avoid being taken in by the end, should the offensive man attempt to do so. Meanwhile, the linebacker will charge the tackle and play him exactly as described above for the defensive tackle.

If the offense is alert, this variation in alignment usually tips off the fact that the cross charge will be used. To avoid this occasionally, both men should play a normal straight away game from this alignment. When the normal charge is being used, the

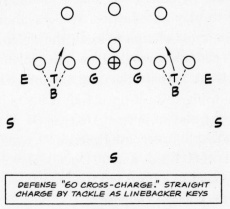

DEFENSE "60 CROSS-CHARGE." STRAIGHT
CHARGE BY TACKLE AS LINEBACKER KEYS

Figure 47

linebacker keys the block of the offensive end and offensive tackle as his tackle shoots through the gap between the two men. If one of the two offensive linemen does not block the tackle, he will be "home free" and in a position to stop the ball most effectively. If either the end or the tackle block the shooting tackle, the linebacker has an excellent key. If the end blocks in, the linebacker moves to the outside. If the tackle blocks out, the linebacker moves to the inside. This key enables the linebacker to support his tackle quickly and accurately.

The slight change in alignment of Defense 60 Cross Charge, together with the three charges of the tackles and linebackers, complicates to a considerable degree the problem of the offensive team. Even though the defense looks like a "stunt set," it is possible to play an effective, straight ahead game. When the cross charge is used, the defense which results is actually an eight-man line evolving from a six-man front. Perhaps the most advantageous single factor in using this set-up is that it alters in so few respects the play of normal Defense 60. If the team has been taught to execute Defense 60, together with the stunts of 60 Inside and 60 Outside, it will be very easy for them to adjust and play the three patterns of 60 Cross Charge Defense.

TIGHT TACKLE 60

The remaining variation of 60 Defense is known as the Tight Tackle 60. Again the ends, guards, and three safety men play regular Defense 60. The only real adjustments involve the tackles and the linebackers. (It is necessary, however, for the defensive ends to alter their charge slightly.)

In playing 60 Tight, the defensive tackles move in and play on the outside shoulder of the offensive tackle. Their assignment is to charge hard into the offensive tackle, control him, and knock him back,

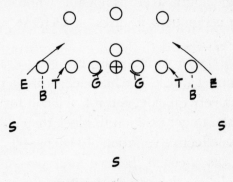

DEFENSE "60 TIGHT"
Figure 48

meanwhile being positive that they are never *blocked out* by the offensive tackle. The tackle should be under control as he charges in order to maintain his ability to move laterally after making contact. If he overcharges and penetrates too far, he will find it difficult to adjust quickly to his angle of pursuit.

Each linebacker takes his position directly in front of the offensive end. He plays the end, keying him exactly as he would the tackle when playing regular Defense 60. If the tackle drives out at him, he should step in and hit the tackle, being positive that the tackle *never blocks him in.*

While the linebacker is playing the end in this

manner, the defensive end should line up normally. However, as the ball is snapped, the end should charge hard to the inside on a course directly at the offensive fullback. He should force the play as quickly and aggressively as possible while executing the same assignment he uses on Defense 54. (See Chapter 9.)

This defensive variation is very good against an inside running attack. The linebackers are in position to support very quickly, and it is difficult for any offensive man to get position to block them. Thus, 60 Tight is an effective variation of Defense 60.

If you, as a coach, believe your personnel can handle only one defensive plan, it would be well to teach Defense 60. With its variations it is probably the most effective, adaptable, most easily learned and played alignment in modern football.

13

Defense 53

Defense 53 is another of the five-man containing unit defenses. The utilization of personnel in this alignment does not require any additional fundamental execution on the part of any player of the team except that the defensive left end must, in this set-up, react somewhat similarly to a linebacker. Therefore, it is necessary that he have a little additional practice and drilling for his new position.

The assignments for Defense 53 are as follows: *Left tackle and right end:* Line up 2 feet outside the offensive end. Be in a three-point stance. Turn in slightly so that you face the offensive fullback. As the ball is snapped, charge hard at a spot approximately 1 yard in front of the fullback. React normally as you make this charge. (1) If the ball is coming your way, continue on your normal angle, flattening a little if a lineman is leading the play. (2) If the play goes away from you, get depth and

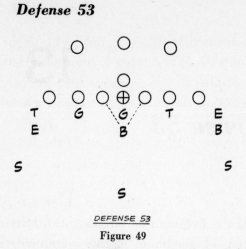

<u>DEFENSE 53</u>
Figure 49

become the leverage man. (3) If a drop-back pass develops, deepen your charge and maintain outside leverage on the passer.

Left guard and right tackle: Line up head up with the offensive tackle. As the ball is snapped, charge hard at the tackle attempting to knock him back. Never let the tackle block you out. Try to keep him on the line of scrimmage so he cannot get downfield to block. It is vitally important that you watch your normal key of the offensive end, offensive tackle, and offensive guard. React to their movements as you would in the "3 on 1" and "5 on 2" drills discussed earlier. (1) If the offensive guard is blocking your teammate playing over the center, and if your tackle is not giving you much opposition, close quickly to the inside and play for a trap. (2) If you are being

138

double teamed by the end and tackle, fight quickly to the outside. It is extremely important that you use your peripheral vision and adjust quickly to the movement of these three offensive men who comprise your key.

Right guard: Line up 1 foot off the line of scrimmage and head up with the offensive center. Drive hard at the center to knock him back. Avoid letting the center cut you to either side alone. React to your key of the center and the two offensive guards. (Same as "3-on-1" drill.) Adjust quickly on the proper angle of pursuit, moving to the ball.

Middle linebacker: Line up about a foot behind your guard. Key the two offensive guards. If you have trouble seeing both guards from this depth, line up a little further back until you can see and react to both of them. (1) If the play to be run is any kind of trap over the center, one guard will block in on the man over the center while the other guard pulls to trap. When this movement occurs, you should shoot very shallowly just past the power block close to your own guard in order to avoid being trapped by the pulling guard. (2) If both guards pull one way or the other, play your key and move with them. (3) If both guards make a pass-protection block, drop back and play for a pass. (4) The most difficult reaction and adjustment develops when both guards fire out at you. This will happen on many straight ahead running plays. When both guards move out at you, try to move quickly, laterally, in the direction of the ball. This will help you to avoid the block of the guard who will be coming out to block you.

With a little practice, the middle guard should be able to execute the keys as described above. If he can execute them well, this defense is most effective.

Outside linebackers: Line up about 1½ feet behind your own tackle and end. Look through the offensive end to the ball. If it is necessary to widen your position slightly to execute this assignment, do so. As the ball is snapped, play the ball exactly as you would if you were a regular defensive end. However, as you react to the ball, react also to the block of the offensive end. (1) If the end blocks out on your end, shoot the gap very quickly. By making this charge, you will quickly close the only really vulnerable hole in the defense. (2) If the end comes downfield, hit him and knock him to the inside. Then react normally to the ball.

As you hit the end when he starts downfield, be conscious of the movement of the ball. If a drop back pass is developing, give ground quickly back and to the outside. Your pass coverage zone will be the flat zone to your outside.

The three safety men react on this defense exactly

as they do on all five-man containing unit alignments.

This defense is adaptable to the use of a series of stunts which complicate, to a tremendous degree, the offensive blocking assignments. The stunts also help make the defense more sound against a team which throws the ball the majority of the time. Through these variations of charge an excellent combination of a hard rush together with a pattern of adequate coverage of passes can be achieved.

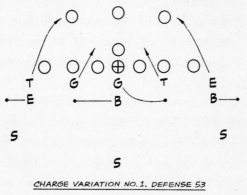

CHARGE VARIATION NO. 1. DEFENSE 53

Figure 50

The most commonly used stunts are cross charges between the tackles and ends on the outside together with a cross charge by the middle guard and middle linebacker over the center. Let us consider these defensive variations in detail.

All men line up exactly as they do on regular Defense 53. *The left tackle and right end* widen their angle of charge and, instead of going for a spot a yard in front of the fullback, they should go for a spot just inside the offensive halfback. They make no attempt to hit the offensive ends while moving on this angle, but should the ends move across their path, they will, of course, hit them, delay them, and continue to drive through as quickly as possible to their point of attack. While moving on this angle, they will react to the key of the ball exactly as they do on any defense.

The right tackle and left guard will line up normally, but instead of charging at the offensive tackle, will shoot the gap hard between the offensive guard and tackle, and go directly at the fullback. While making this charge it is vitally important that both men watch the offensive guard on their side. (1) If the guard double teams with his center on the middle guard, the tackle and left guard must quickly flatten their angle of charge and keep their heads inside the trapping man, thereby avoiding the trap block. This charge is vulnerable to a well-executed trap if the tackles play carelessly. The trap will not be successful if the tackles do a good job of keying the guard. (2) If the guard turns out, the defensive man should again flatten his charge quickly so that he cannot be turned out.

If the tackle and guard do a good job of *keying the guard,* the defense will be successful. If they charge blindly, the defense is vulnerable down the middle.

The right guard and middle linebacker both become linebackers on this defensive variation. Both of them move out and back to support against off-tackle runs and to cover the hook-pass zone. As the ball is snapped, the linebacker takes two steps rapidly to one side or the other. (The middle guard will move in the opposite direction.) Having done so, he reacts normally to the ball. As he makes this move, he should *key the guard* on his side exactly as he would in regular Defense 53. If the movement of the guard indicates that he is moving in the wrong direction, he should adjust quickly in accordance with the movement of the offensive guard. If the guard has made a pass-protection block, the linebacker should deepen and cover the hook zone.

The middle guard will move back and out at the snap of the ball and cover to the side opposite the middle linebacker. As he makes this move, he too must watch the movement of the offensive guard. He should key the guard exactly as the linebacker keys him. (1) If the guard is blocking in on him, he should, of course, fight the pressure of the block and control as well as possible in his immediate area.

(2) If the guard is pulling away from his movement, he should stop and move with the guard. (3) If the guard makes a pass-protection block, the middle guard will continue back and out to cover the hook zone on his side.

The outside linebackers have complete outside responsibility on this defense. At the snap of the ball, both of them should take two steps to the outside and then react normally as defensive ends to the pattern of the play. (1) If the ball is coming their way, they should continue to the outside, staying in position in order to come up and turn the play in should a run develop. (2) If the ball goes away from them, they should retreat quickly, keeping outside position on every man of the offensive team. (3) If a drop back pass develops, they should continue to drop into the flat to cover that zone *and should remain in position to cover any screen pass thrown to their side.*

This defensive variation combines a very strong outside rush by the end and tackle with excellent short pass coverage since the middle guard and middle linebacker are covering the hook zones very quickly, and the two outside linebackers are covering the flat zones almost with the snap of the ball. The hard outside rush by the ends and tackles should come as a surprise to the offensive team and may be

effective in getting a man through to the passer before he can throw the ball.

The second defensive variation from Defense 53 is
based on an outside charge by the tackle. The theory of this variation is to have a complete change of
pace against the offensive team. The pass coverage
remains almost as good as it was on the first variation outlined above, but the rush, instead of coming
from the outside, comes from the inside.

The assignments are as follows:

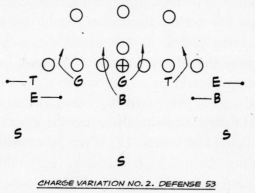

CHARGE VARIATION NO. 2. DEFENSE 53

Figure 51

Left guard and right tackle: Line up as you normally would for Defense 53. As the ball is snapped,
shoot hard to your outside through the gap between
the end and the offensive tackle. Continue on this
angle until you are *sure you can keep leverage* on the
ball. If the play goes away from you, deepen quickly

and get in position to stop any delayed reverses. As you make this charge, work for deep penetration quickly and cleanly. Remember, you are the *outside leverage man*.

Right guard and middle linebacker: Cross charge over the inside shoulders of the two offensive guards. It makes no difference which man goes to the right or which man goes to the left. The right guard should line up about 2 to 2½ feet off the line of scrimmage so that he will have room enough to get past the center even though the center beats him to the charge. The middle linebacker should line up close behind the guard. As the guard makes his cross charge he should key the offensive guard. His angle of charge should be at the inside shoulder of the guard. (1) If the guard is blocking in on him, he should flatten immediately so that the guard will not be able to block him in. (2) If the guard pulls in the same direction as he is shooting, he should flatten his charge and chase the play. (3) If the guard pulls in the opposite direction, he should immediately change his angle of charge and move with the offensive guard.

The linebacker shoots at the inside shoulder of the opposite guard and keys the guard normally. Both the right guard and the middle linebacker should remember that they are working for penetration and that if a drop back pass develops they must rush the passer.

While these four inside men are rushing on the angles described, the *left tackle* and the *right end* line up normally for Defense 53. As the ball is snapped, both men take two steps to the outside. (1) If the ball starts toward them, they come up quickly maintaining outside leverage. (2) If the ball goes away, they turn and drop straight back, reacting as a member of the containing unit of the defense. (3) If a drop back pass develops, they fall off to cover the flat zone, protecting also against any flat or screen pass to their side.

The two outside linebackers take their positions normally. As the ball is snapped, both men take one step to the inside being sure that the offensive end cannot block them out. As they make this charge, they key the ball. (1) If the ball is moving on a running pattern, they react normally as linebackers, chasing the play if it is going away from them and moving in to meet the play if it is coming to their side. (2) If a drop back pass develops, they drop back and to the inside to cover their hook zones.

These two stunts make Defense 53 truly effective against a pass attack. They provide excellent coverage since only four men are rushing while seven men are dropping back to cover. Perhaps the greatest strength of the two stunts is that in one instance a hard four-man rush develops from the *outside,* while in the next instance the strong four-man rush develops from *inside.* This variation in the area from which the pressure will come to rush the passer oftentimes confuses the pass-protection blocking.

One additional stunt is needed—that of having all five linemen and the three linebackers rush together so that eight men penetrate at the ball as soon as it is snapped. This "Red Dog" charge forces the issue quickly and puts terrific pressure on the passer.

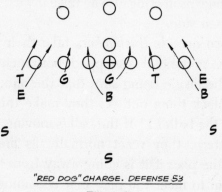

"RED DOG" CHARGE. DEFENSE 53

Figure 52

When "Red Dog" is called, the middle guard and linebacker cross charge, the outside linebackers shoot the gap between the end and tackle, and the left guard and right tackle drive through the inside shoulder of the tackle.

Defense 53, played normally and with the three variations described, is a very well-balanced defense. It is only strong as a forcing defense when the eight-man rush is used, but it is a sound containing defense in every other instance. If the stunts are used accurately, and if, while stunting, the defensive men will *key properly,* the effectiveness of the forcing portion of the defense is materially improved. If the forcing portion occasionally can force errors and hold opponents to no gain or short gains, the defense will be the soundest of all alignments, since the containing portion of the defense played well is always adequate to stop the long run or long pass.

To complete our discussion of this defense we should go over the adjustments that must be made against flankers. The rules are very simple and correspond very closely with those given for adjustments to flankers for a five-man containing defense.

The rules for adjustment to flankers are: (1) If the end flankers, the linebacker on that side will drop off and out and play the end exactly as was described in Chapter 6 on containing defenses. (2) If the on halfback or fullback flankers, the outside linebacker drops off and plays exactly as described in the previous chapter. (3) If the opposite halfback crosses so that the offensive formation becomes unbalanced, the outside linebacker will play as a defensive end.

Defense 53

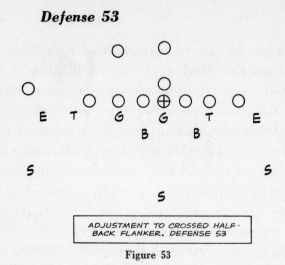

ADJUSTMENT TO CROSSED HALF-
BACK FLANKER. DEFENSE 53

Figure 53

In this instance the two remaining linebackers will move over and play just inside of the defensive tackles. This will make the middle of the defense correspond to Defense 72. Both linebackers now key their respective guards exactly as they would in Defense 72.

14

Defense 70

Defense 70 is, in most particulars, very similar to Defense 53. However, from the alignment, it is possible to get variations of stunts which require difficult blocking adjustments for the offensive team.

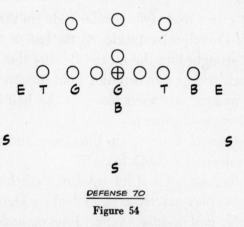

DEFENSE 70

Figure 54

Basic Defense 70 is played as follows:

Ends: Line up on the line of scrimmage 2½ feet

outside the offensive ends. React exactly as you would in Defense 60.

Left tackle and fullback (right linebacker): Take your position head up with the offensive end. Charge straight into the end. Hit him, control him, and be sure he cannot block you in. (1) If the play goes away from you, get deep quickly so that you are as deep as the ball and are in position to stop any delayed reverse. You are the leverage man. (2) If the play comes your way, react normally in pursuit along the line of scrimmage. (3) If a drop back pass develops, the left tackle will rush, but the fullback will drop out of the line and cover the hook-pass zone on his side.

Left guard and right tackle: Line up directly in front of the offensive tackle. As the ball is snapped, charge straight into the tackle. Be sure that he cannot block you in. Control him, hold him on the line of scrimmage, and then move to the ball on your normal angle of pursuit.

Right guard: Line up on the center and play exactly as described for Defense 53.

Middle linebacker: Line up directly behind your guard and play exactly as described for Defense 53.

Outside and middle safeties: Line up and play as you normally would on all five-man containing defense.

Stunts from Defense 70 add greatly to the effectiveness of the defense. The two standard stunts are 70 Inside and 70 Outside.

70 INSIDE

All men on the line of scrimmage line up exactly as described for Defense 70. On the snap of the ball they charge as follows:

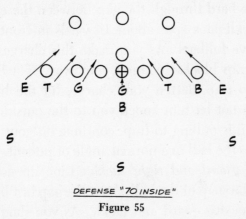

DEFENSE "70 INSIDE"

Figure 55

Ends: Drive hard directly at the offensive fullback. Even though the play is coming your way, continue on this course endeavoring to hit the blockers and knock them back into the backfield. Keep closing until the ball is at least as wide as you are. At this point, if the ball is going around you, give ground to the outside. But never anticipate that the ball will go around you. If you do, you will open up a tremendous gap between yourself and your tackle. This opening will be so big that it will be virtually impossible for your linebacker or your tackle to recover quickly enough to stop the play. Remember, penetrate until the ball is parallel with you, at which time you may begin to retreat with the ball carrier to the outside.

Left tackle and fullback: Line up normally. Charge hard through the gap between the end and the tackle at a spot about 1½ yards in front of the offensive fullback. As you make this charge, watch for a trap blocker coming your way. If a lineman pulls to trap, flatten your charge, hit the lineman, and do not let him knock you to the outside. If no lineman is pulling to trap, continue on your course, react to the ball in a normal angle of pursuit.

Left guard and right tackle: Line up normally. With the snap of the ball, shoot the gap fast between the offensive guard and tackle. As you shoot, react to the movement of the offensive guard exactly as described for the second stunt of Defense 53.

Right guard: Line up 2 feet off the line of scrimmage head up with the offensive center. Charge hard one out of four times, play soft the other three times. Be sure the center does not cut you alone to either side.

Middle linebacker: Deepen and play about 2

yards behind the defensive guard. Key the guard exactly as you would in Defense 53. Be sure that you have depth enough so that you can move laterally to the area outside of the offensive end to either side before either offensive guard can come straight through to cut you off. You have no inside responsibility on this defense. Key the guard and move quickly to the outside, being positive that neither guard blocks you in.

The three safety men react normally as on all five-man containing defenses.

70 OUTSIDE

This defense is exactly opposite in charge to 70 Inside. Assignments are as follows:

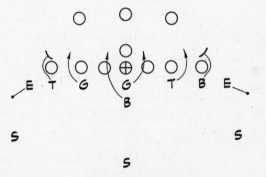

DEFENSE "70 OUTSIDE"

Figure 56

Ends: Line up normally. As the ball is snapped, take two steps back and to the outside. From this position react as you normally would in Defense 60 as a member of the five-man containing unit.

Left tackle and linebacker: Line up shading the inside of the offensive end. As the ball is snapped, charge hard across the face of the offensive end, being sure that the end does not block you in. Attempt to hit the end, but be sure you can get past him to the outside. As soon as you have cleared the end and recovered your balance, play normal defense. If the play is coming your way, move back to the inside and on a normal angle of pursuit. You do not have outside or inside leverage; you simply are protecting the area outside the offensive end. If the play is going away from you, deepen. You are the leverage man against all reverses.

Left guard and right tackle: Line up head up with the offensive tackle. As the ball is snapped, charge hard to the outside through the gap between the offensive end and tackle. As soon as you have made penetration, recover your balance and face straight upfield. React on a normal angle of pursuit.

Right guard and middle linebacker: Cross charge all of the time on this defense. Take your position and play exactly as described for 53 Inside.

There is one other stunt which may be used effectively from this alignment. It can be combined with either 70 Inside or 70 Outside. This stunt involves a cross charge between the end and the offensive tackle. To execute it, the end and tackle line up exactly as they would for regular Defense 70. The ends charge fast and hard directly at the offensive quarterback. They continue to penetrate and force the play unless the ball is going away from them or a drop back pass develops. In either of these instances they deepen quickly to get and maintain outside position on the ball. Remember, the main objective is to charge shallow, fast, and hard in an effort to get to the ball before the play is organized.

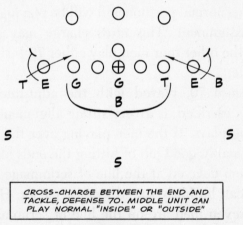

CROSS-CHARGE BETWEEN THE END AND TACKLE, DEFENSE 70. MIDDLE UNIT CAN PLAY NORMAL "INSIDE" OR "OUTSIDE"

Figure 57

As the end charges on the course indicated, the tackle will move laterally two steps down the line of scrimmage. As soon as he clears his end, the tackle will take one step across the line of scrimmage and then react as a normal end.

Note: In making this adjustment it is well to have the tackle and end exchange positions before the snap of the ball. When this is done, neither of them has a new assignment to learn. The end will be playing over the offensive end in the tackle's usual position before the ball is snapped, but after completing his stunt he will be in his regular position and can react in his normal manner. The tackle will appear to be an end at the start of the play, but after charging on the angle described above, he, too, will be in his normal position and will be playing his regular assignment. This cross charge may be used while the other four men play either 70 Inside or 70 Outside.

Defense 70, played with the adjustments and stunts described, is a very strong alignment against running plays. If the men playing over the ends do a reasonably good job of hitting the ends and keeping them delayed at the line of scrimmage, the defense can be fairly sound against passes. However, since seven men are on the line of scrimmage, the alignment is necessarily handicapped in covering quick hook pass plays.

15

Goal Line Defenses

The theory of goal line defense is exactly opposite to that of the normal defensive pattern used out on the field. When the ball is not close to the goal line, short gains do not materially hurt the defensive team. Close to the goal line one or two short gains may result in a score. Because of this fact, the two types of defense are entirely different.

The basic difference between the normal defense and goal line defense evolves from the following factors: When the ball is inside the defensive team's 10 yard line, there is no depth of field to defend. The only area remaining on the field of play is the 10 yards to the goal line plus the 10 yards to the end zone, a distance of 20 yards. Normally, no defensive player needs to be dropped back farther than the goal line, even on pass plays, as the ball cannot get to an offensive pass receiver before he will be out of bounds if it is thrown high enough to be over the heads of defensive secondary men playing on the goal line. Since there is *no depth to defend,* the entire eleven men of the defensive team can *force* the issue with the offensive team quickly.

When the ball is in the goal line area, a short gain will probably result in a score. When this happens, the defense, of course, has failed completely. When the ball is out of the field of play, short gains result only in first downs and even though short gains do result repeatedly, the defense has not failed in their major objective. If the offense is always held to the short gain they usually will commit an error and lose the ball before they can score.

On the field of play, in order to have good pursuit on the part of the defensive team, none of the linemen should penetrate unless a stunt is called which makes it necessary for them to try to do so. If the linemen do penetrate and the ball happens to go to some area other than the particular spot they are shooting for, they will lose the effectiveness of their pursuit. Therefore, out on the field of play most linemen in most defenses are taught to hit, to control, to stay on the line of scrimmage, and then to slide to the ball as quickly as possible and at the best angle of pursuit. On the goal line, pursuit is not much help to the defensive team because a short gain which is stopped by pursuit will still result in a touchdown.

Therefore, the defensive linemen in a goal line defense alter their play completely. On the goal line they must try to penetrate as quickly and as deeply as possible into the opponent's backfield. If they can get this penetration, they will stop the play for a loss or at least for no gain. The defense will have been successful. *The basic difference between normal and goal line defenses is the charge of the defensive line.* Out on the field they are hitting, sliding, and pursuing, while on the goal line they are charging low and hard, working for penetration.

The basic difficulty in developing an adequate goal line defense is a result of the necessity for some of the individuals on the defensive team to learn additional, individual defensive fundamentals. All men who are on the line of scrimmage in a goal line defense are working for penetration. They must know how to charge and to react as linemen. Seven, eight, or nine men, depending on the set-up used, must learn to execute the low, hard, penetrating charge. This means that at least two, and possibly three or four men, must learn this additional fundamental. Luckily, the difficulty of learning it is tempered somewhat by the fact that, as they charge, the defensive linemen do not have much chance to react to the movement of the offensive team. On a goal line defense the linemen, instead of charging with a controlled movement, hitting, and then finding the ball and sliding to it, merely charge as low and aggressively as possible, working for penetration. Any charge that does not involve reaction after the start of the charge is much easier to learn quickly than is a controlled charge which involves additional reactions and adjustments.

When a goal line defense is used, it is best for the men on the line of scrimmage, who are working for penetration, to take a four-point stance. This is a fundamental change of stance, but since it is absolutely necessary to gain penetration if the defense is to succeed, the best stance for penetrating should be used. In this stance the feet are a little further back and the hands and arms are a little more extended than is the case in the normal defensive stance. Most of the body's weight should be carried by the hands. As the charge is made, the hands should shoot out ahead, forcing an opening. The shoulders are driven straight ahead hard, but in no case should the shoulders be raised. The charge is really a lunge. After extending the body with the full use of the back and leg muscles, the feet should be brought forward as rapidly as possible and the defensive man should regain his balance as he scrambles and fights for further penetration. (*See Illustrations No. 16 and 17.*)

There are a number of alignments which can be

Illustration No. 16. Four-point stance for linemen on goal line charge.

Illustration No. 17. Goal line charge between two men, showing penetration.

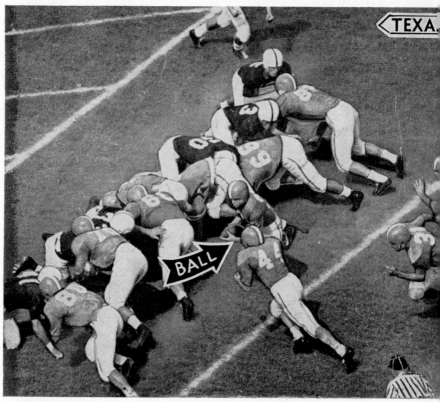

Illustration No. 18. A goal line charge vs. the University of Texas.

Illustration No. 19. The crashing-end—looping-tackle stunt by Oklahoma men results in a loss for Oklahoma State.

Illustration No. 20. Oklahoma tacklers show the great determination necessary for defensive success as they close in on a North Carolina University ball carrier.

Illustration No. 21. Great skill in playing the ball, as it is thrown, enables Jerry Tubbs to intercept a pass against the University of Texas.

used successfully on the goal line. Since the quarter-back sneak is one of football's best short yardage scoring plays, we believe the eight-man goal line defense is perhaps the most effective. This alignment does a reasonably good job of stopping the quarter-back sneak play. The alignment is played as follows:

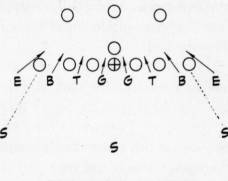

EIGHT-MAN GOAL LINE DEFENSE

Figure 58

Guards: Line up in the gap on either side of the center. Charge low and hard through the gap, achieving penetration as deeply and as quickly as possible. As you penetrate, make every effort to get a hand, an arm, or a shoulder to the quarterback before he can move straight ahead or laterally to your outside.

Tackles: Line up in the gap between the offensive guard and offensive tackle. As the ball is snapped, charge hard through the gap and work for penetration. If you are fortunate enough to gain penetration, react to the ball as quickly as possible. Remember, do not charge into either of the offensive linemen. Try to penetrate *the gap area* between the linemen in order to get into the backfield.

Linebackers: Line up in the gap between the offensive end and tackle. As the ball is snapped, shoot the gap moving on an inside angle. Work for penetration. Play the ball.

Ends: Line up in a three-point stance about 1½ yards outside the offensive end. As the ball is snapped, charge hard past the hip of the offensive end for a spot about 1½ yards in front of the fullback. Continue on this course and attempt to close the gap between yourself and your linebacker. You have *no outside responsibility.* Your assignment is to eliminate the hole between yourself and your linebacker. If the ball goes away from you, deepen and become the leverage man. If the ball drops back for a forward pass play, deepen your angle of charge and keep leverage on the passer.

Outside safety men: Outside safeties usually key the movement of the ball. On this goal line defense, as you key the movement of the ball, watch the offensive end. Put yourself in position so you can look through the end to the ball. If the end blocks hard to the inside, come up quickly outside of your end.

Force the play and turn it to the inside. If the end comes downfield, drop back with him, maintaining outside position and deep position on him so that you can cover him if he breaks into your zone on a forward pass. Be sure that you watch the end and make your reaction as a result of his movement. If the end is downfield, the linebacker and defensive end can probably maintain outside leverage on any running play. If the end blocks, you must come up quickly, since this additional block gives added strength to the end run.

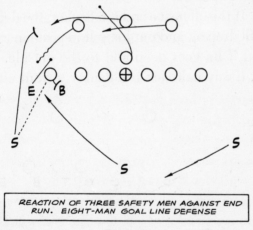

REACTION OF THREE SAFETY MEN AGAINST END RUN. EIGHT-MAN GOAL LINE DEFENSE

Figure 59

Middle safety: Line up about 4 yards deep. React to the ball as it is snapped, moving quickly to either side. On running plays you must react fast enough

Goal Line Defenses

to fill the gap between your end and your outside safety. As you move laterally, try to ascertain whether any linemen are downfield. If they are, you can close toward the line of scrimmage as you move laterally. If no linemen are downfield, you should move laterally and back since a pass probably will develop.

ADJUSTMENTS TO FLANKERS IN "8-3" GOAL LINE DEFENSE

The rules for flanker adjustments are very simple and are as follows:

(1) If the offensive end is a flanker, the defensive end will drop off and put himself in position to cover the end if he goes deep and to the outside.

(2) If any halfback is a flanker toward either of

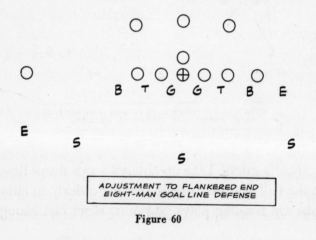

ADJUSTMENT TO FLANKERED END
EIGHT-MAN GOAL LINE DEFENSE

Figure 60

the outside safeties (on halfback, fullback, or crossed halfback), the outside safety man will widen and put himself in position to cover the flanker deep and to the outside.

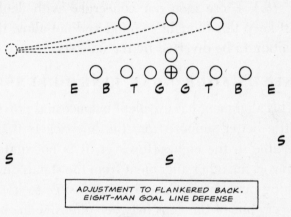

ADJUSTMENT TO FLANKERED BACK.
EIGHT-MAN GOAL LINE DEFENSE

Figure 61

(3) The middle safety will make no adjustment against a flankered end. Against a flankered back the middle safety should move over slightly and play approximately between the offensive guard and the offensive tackle, to the side of the flanker.

These adjustments sound deceptively simple. Actually they are adequate to cover all flanker set-ups on the goal line. Men not involved in adjusting to the flankers must never be deceived by the use of flankers by the offense on the goal line. In this area of the field, most flankers are used to spread and mentally harass the defense. Men not assigned to cover flankers must remember that their paramount duty on all goal line defenses is to charge quickly and powerfully in order to gain penetration. (*See Illustration No. 18.*) Those men not concerned with flankers must keep this thought in mind and not allow their attention to be diverted by the flankers.

SEVEN-FOUR GOAL LINE DEFENSE

This alignment has excellent balance and provides a little better support from the linebackers than is available in the eight. However, it is not quite as strong as the other alignment from the standpoint of gaining penetration since it is impossible to line up in every one of the gaps between offensive linemen. Whenever a defensive lineman on a goal line defense lines up almost in front of an offensive man he limits tremendously the possibility of his gaining quick penetration. On this alignment, the middle guard is placed in this position. The other linemen do have the opportunity of penetrating, but since the middle guard cannot do so, and since the defensive men adjacent to him are one gap away, the defense is somewhat vulnerable to the quarterback sneak and "fullback-drive" plays.

Assignments for seven-four goal line defense are as follows:

Goal Line Defenses

Ends: Line up and play exactly as described for the eight-man line goal line defense.

Left tackle and right linebacker: Line up in the gap between the offensive end and offensive tackle.

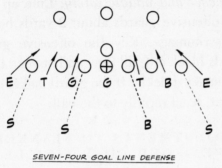

SEVEN-FOUR GOAL LINE DEFENSE

Figure 62

As the ball is snapped, shoot hard across the gap on an angle to the inside. Work for penetration. React to the ball.

Left guard and right tackle: Line up in the gap between the offensive guard and tackle. As the ball is snapped, charge hard through the gap. Work for penetration. Move to the ball.

Right guard: Line up head up with the offensive center in a low four-point stance. As the ball is snapped, charge hard into the center, being positive he cannot raise you up or drive you back. You must be lower than he is in order to knock him back into his own backfield.

169

Goal Line Defenses

Outside safeties: Line up and play exactly as described for the eight-man line goal line defense. Key the offensive end in exactly the same way. You must react *to the end* as you react to the ball.

Linebacker and middle safety: Line up just outside the offensive guards about 2 yards behind the line of scrimmage. Key the offensive guards. If the guards block out, fill the gap between the guard and the center quickly. If the guard makes any other movement, react rapidly to the ball.

ADJUSTMENTS TO FLANKERS IN SEVEN-FOUR GOAL LINE DEFENSE

(1) *Outside safeties:* If the end or any back flankers to your side, widen, deepen, and put yourself in position to cover him deep and to the outside.

(2) *Linebacker and middle safety:* (a) If a back

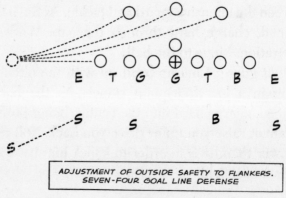

ADJUSTMENT OF OUTSIDE SAFETY TO FLANKERS.
SEVEN-FOUR GOAL LINE DEFENSE

Figure 63

flankers to the opposite side, make no adjustment.
(b) If a back flankers to your side, deepen one step,
and if a pass shows, drop quickly to your outside.
Be sure that the end does not cross in front of

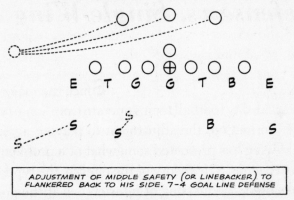

ADJUSTMENT OF MIDDLE SAFETY (OR LINEBACKER) TO
FLANKERED BACK TO HIS SIDE. 7-4 GOAL LINE DEFENSE

Figure 64

you. You must cover the end from the inside. Remember to key the offensive guard. If the guard
makes a pass protection block, drop quickly to the
hook zone. Be in position to cover the end if he
hooks or if he breaks on an angle to the inside.

The principles of goal line defense remain the
same regardless of the alignment used. The majority
of the team becomes a forcing unit. The linemen do
not hit, control, or pursue. Rather, they penetrate
between offensive linemen. The "containing men"
line up closer to the ball and use a key which enables them to join the forcing unit almost immediately after the ball is snapped.

171

16

Defense vs. Single-Wing

Since the majority of present-day football teams operate from some type of "T" formation, the adjustment to playing against single-wing has presented somewhat of a problem to many coaches. The theory of the offense, the types of blocks used, the massing of interference at the point of attack, all of which are characteristic of the single-wing, differ greatly from "T" formation offensive football.

Yet, a team usually has only one week of practice, to make the transition from the defense used against the "T" formation to the defense against single-wing. In this short space of practice time we believe it is difficult to change, to any great degree, the basic concept and fundamental moves of the defense. If too many adjustments are tried they probably will not be well executed because there simply is not enough time in a week's practice to learn many radically different moves and reactions. In addition, a *psychological loss* occurs if the players in trying to learn too many new things develop a tendency to lose confidence in their ability to cope with the new attack. When this happens they feel inadequately prepared for the game.

An important part of playing successful defense is the confidence on the part of each man that the offensive team cannot score. If the week's practice in preparation for a single-wing team has been devoted to making tremendous adjustments in stance, charge, keys, and the other basic elements of defense, it is possible that the team will feel the new attack is too tricky and difficult to stop. This will cause them to lose the confidence necessary to play effectively on defense.

Actually, it is best not to "panic" in any sense in preparing for a single-wing team. The best approach is to adjust a defense that the team already knows.

When playing against a single-wing attack, most coaches believe their defensive linemen should operate a great deal lower than is necessary against the "T" formation. Since most blocks on the single-wing attack are "double teams," and since the trap blocks are delivered low and hard and from an excellent angle, it definitely helps to have the defensive linemen play low and charge hard so that they avoid being driven back. There is real merit in this concept. However, if an attempt is made radically to alter the defensive charge during the week of the game, the linemen probably will not be able to learn to execute it well. If they do not learn well, the lack of confidence described above may result.

For a number of years the University of Oklahoma went through this pattern of coaching in preparation for single-wing teams. A rope was brought out on the practice field the first day of the week. Linemen were instructed to charge beneath the rope, and, after learning to do so reasonably well, were taught to charge underneath the rope and then hit dummies placed just opposite the rope. To climax the preparation in charging low, actual "3-on-1" and "5-on-2" defensive drills (see Chapter 4 on line fundamentals) were used with all men drilling underneath the ropes. In reflection, after a fair analysis of the results, this practice did not seem to accomplish anything except to develop doubts on the part of the defensive players in their ability to cope with this different formation.

Since the players seemed to worry so much after this type of practice, our coaching staff decided that the next time we met a single-wing team we would play them, in all fundamental respects, exactly the same as if they were a "T" formation team. We would simply adjust one or two of the defenses which our team already knew and believed in. When we did this, our players seemed to regain their defensive confidence. In our opinion, our defense against single-wing has been at least thirty to forty per cent more effective as a result of this plan than it was when we tried to convince our team that they were meeting a totally new and different problem.

In order to play a defense well the fundamentals should be learned during the spring and fall pre-season practice. These fundamentals should not be altered during the season. There is never enough practice time available from game to game to learn radically different assignments. Therefore, in meeting a single-wing, we believe it best to use techniques already learned and mastered.

DEFENSE 72 VS. SINGLE-WING

This defense is an adaptation of Defense 72 as used against the "T" formation. All men line up in their same relative positions. The secondary unit rotates exactly as they would against a crossed flanker. The actual assignments are as follows:

Left end (corner man rotated up): Line up on the line of scrimmage 3 feet outside the wingback. Look through the wingback to the fullback and tailback. Use your normal rule of "Ball come, I come; ball go, I go," but, as you play this key, you must always be

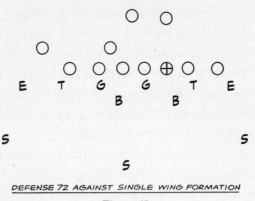

DEFENSE 72 AGAINST SINGLE WING FORMATION

Figure 65

conscious of the movement of the wingback. When the ball is snapped, take one step across the line of scrimmage, watching the wingback. If the ball is coming your way and the wingback is swinging to get outside position on you, take one more step in and then fade with the wingback so that he *can never block you in*. This is a most difficult block. If you will take two steps across the line of scrimmage and then give ground to the outside, the wingback should never be able to hook you in. But if you look at only the fullback and the tailback and lose sight of the wingback, he will be able to hit you while you are "blind" and will be able to block you effectively.

If the wingback drives straight downfield, or double teams in on the tackle and the ball is coming your

176

way, flatten your course quickly and move to the inside to close the gap between yourself and the tackle. Continue to close and be in position to meet the blockers with a strong shoulder shiver. As you hit the blockers, maintain your ability to move back and to the outside. Your basic responsibility is *never to become blocked in* by any member of the offensive team. If you watch the wingback, you will not be blocked in by him. However, if you drive in too hard when the wingback goes straight upfield, one of the linemen, the fullback, or the blocking back may be able to hook you. Remember, close the gap fast, but maintain your balance well enough so that you can adjust and move back to the outside if necessary.

If the ball goes away from you, turn and drop back. Play as a normal end of a five-man containing unit.

Left tackle: Line up just outside the offensive end, facing slightly to the inside. Watch the end-wingback combination. As the ball is snapped, charge hard at the offensive end. Never let the end hook you in alone. As you charge the end, be conscious of the wingback. (1) If he is double teaming on you, be sure that you can recover off the end and hit the wingback with a good forearm or hand shiver while working to the outside. If the wingback blocks you in, you have not failed in your assignment. However, you should make every effort to fight through the pressure of his block to the outside. (2) If the end blocks to the inside on your guard, work fast down the line of scrimmage to the inside. Do not get penetration if the end makes this movement. In all probability, the blocking back or a lineman will trap you. (3) If the ball goes away from you, get depth immediately until you are as deep as the ball. Maintain outside leverage against reverses.

Left guard: Line up shading the outside of the offensive tackle. As the ball is snapped, charge hard into the tackle, being sure that he cannot block you in alone. As you make the charge, use your usual peripheral vision in keying the three offensive linemen in your immediate area. If either the end or middle guard is driving at you, adjust your charge to meet the pressure of the block. Play the ball.

Note: You must be conscious of the fact that the only likely trap against you will be from the inside. If you charge across the line of scrimmage, hit the guard opposite you, and get past him too easily, you should suspect that a trap play is being run. When this happens, turn your head quickly to the inside and drive back for the line of scrimmage. Try to keep your head inside the trap blocker, who, in this instance, will either be the short side tackle or the guard playing next to the offensive center.

Right guard: Line up head up with the middle lineman. Since this formation usually is played from an unbalanced line you will be opposite the middle guard. Charge straight into the middle guard, control your charge as well as possible, but hit with enough strength to drive the guard back. Use your peripheral vision; watch the tackle, the guard, and the center. React to these three men as you normally would in a regular "3-on-1" drill. If you penetrate too easily you should suspect a trap is in the making. Traps on you will almost always come from your inside (your left). If you feel a trap in the making, do not penetrate further. Turn your head to the inside and move back toward the line of scrimmage.

Right tackle: Line up on the offensive tackle, shading him to the outside. Be positive that he cannot block you in alone. Watch the center, the tackle, and the end. Key these three men exactly as you would on regular "3-on-1" drill. If you get penetration too easily, suspect a trap. The trap will always come from the inside. If you feel a trap coming, do not penetrate into the backfield. Turn your head along the line of scrimmage, and keep your head between the trap blocker and the course of the ball.

Right end: Line up on the outside shoulder of the offensive end. Charge the end and hit him, making every effort to keep him on the line of scrimmage. React to the end's block. If the end is attempting to go downfield, hit him and hold him up. As soon as he gets away from you, move in, reacting normally to the ball with your old rule of "Ball come, I come; ball go, I go." You must remember that the end should never be allowed to get off the line of scrimmage *to your outside*. If he is able to do this, he will be able to hook you in. Your basic assignment is never to be blocked in by the offensive end.

If the end blocks in on your tackle, move down the line of scrimmage with him, trying to knock him off the block. Stay shallow so that you cannot be blocked out by linemen or the blocking back coming your way on a reverse.

If the ball is going away from you, deepen as soon as you lose control of the end. When you are as deep as the ball, pursue it, maintaining leverage on the play.

Left linebacker: Line up 2½ yards deep head up with the outside guard. You must play a little deeper against single-wing than you do against the "T" formation. There are two reasons for doing this: first, on single-wing plays the ball will be thrown by the center approximately 4 to 5 yards back to the fullback or the tailback. These men must bring the ball forward and the resulting time element in getting the ball to the line of scrimmage will give you a better opportunity to diagnose the play and move to it than you have against the "T" formation. Since single-wing plays hit more slowly than do "T" formation plays, you do not need to be quite as close to the line of scrimmage to meet the play at the line of scrimmage.

The second reason why you should play deeper is that the double-team blocking and strong interference formed by pulling linemen may drive the defensive linemen farther back than is the case against a "T" formation. Double team blocks usually are able to force defensive linemen back off the line of scrimmage. If you, as a linebacker, play too close to the line of scrimmage, you may be trapped by one of these double-team blocks driving one of your own linemen back into your area so that you lose your ability to move laterally. It is wise to be lined up deep enough so that you will not be cut off by successful double-team blocks and lose your ability to move on your normal and desired angle of pursuit.

React to the guard exactly as you would in a regular "T" formation. If the guard pulls either way, go with him. If the guard makes an aggressive block to either side, start to fill the hole. Be conscious of the linemen on either side of your guard. If either of these men pulls in either direction, do not continue through the hole. Move with them. If neither of them pulls, continue to fill the gap. The ball will be coming into your area. If the guard makes a pass-protection block, drop quickly to the hook zone.

Right linebacker: Take your depth 2½ yards behind the line of scrimmage. Line up shading the short side of the defensive center (you must be deeper than you would be against a "T" formation for the reasons given above). React to the offensive center exactly as you would to the offensive guard in a "T" formation. If the center pulls in either direction, go with him. If the center blocks aggressively to the right or to the left, come up to fill the hole. Be conscious of the offensive linemen on either side of the center. If neither of these men has pulled, continue to shoot through the gap. If either of them has pulled, do not continue through the gap. Adjust, play slowly, find the ball, and react on your normal angle of pursuit. If the center makes a pass-protection block, drop back and cover your normal hook zone.

Outside safety (on side of the wingback): You should react and play against single-wing exactly as you would against a "T" formation with a crossed halfback.

Defense vs. Single-Wing

The outside safety on the side of the wingback should line up 3 yards outside the wingback and approximately 8 yards deep. As the ball is snapped look through the uncovered lineman to the ball. You should always be playing pass defense first and not be overly worried about the possibility of a run. In most instances the uncovered lineman will give you an excellent key. Remember that you must stay back and play pass until some lineman is down the field or the ball carrier has crossed the line of scrimmage.

Outside safety away from the wingback: Line up 2 to 3 yards outside the offensive end, 6 to 8 yards downfield. Look through the uncovered lineman (in this case the center) to the ball. React normally to the movement of the uncovered lineman. Remember, you must play pass defense first and must not be caught up forcing the play unless you are positive it is a run.

Middle safety: Line up 12 to 15 yards deep, approximately opposite the offensive fullback. Move laterally with the flow of the play. As you make this movement, look at the uncovered lineman. Be sure that you do not come up unless the uncovered lineman is downfield. Your first movement is lateral, and if the lineman is not downfield you should begin to give ground slightly back on your second or third step. If the ball continues in a lateral direction outside the defensive tackle to either side, you should speed up your lateral movement and attempt to get outside position quickly in order that you can call "clear" to your outside halfback. As soon as you are wide and deep enough to cover the deep outside zone, call "clear" so that your outside halfback can move up to cover the flat and support the play. You will have no trouble in doing this if you will slide with the movement of the ball and give ground back and to the outside quickly if the ball continues laterally past the defensive tackles.

STUNTS FROM DEFENSE 72

There are a number of stunts from this defense, all of which are very similar to the stunts diagrammed and explained for Defense 72 against the "T" formation. Since most single-wing teams pull offensive linemen to lead the play, slants and loops on the part of defensive linemen seem to be more effective against the single-wing formation than they are against the "T." Another factor that makes stunts effective is that single-wing plays do not hit quite as quickly as do "T" formation plays. Linemen have a better chance of recovering and pursuing, even though they have started their slant or movement in the wrong direction.

DEFENSE 72 LEFT

In playing this defensive adjustment, all linemen should take their positions almost as they do for Defense 72. They should line up in the same position laterally, but should drop back off the line of scrimmage about a foot to a foot and a half. If they drop too deep, and it is noticeable to the offensive team, it would be better to play on the line of scrimmage. However, if they are only a short distance back off the line, they will have a better chance to complete their stunt before the offensive linemen are able to get to them.

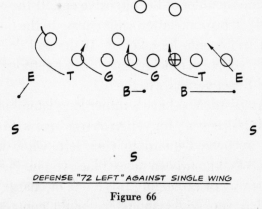

DEFENSE "72 LEFT" AGAINST SINGLE WING

Figure 66

Left end: As the ball is snapped, take two retreating steps back off the line of scrimmage and then react to the ball exactly as you would in normal circumstances. Play as a corner man against a "T" formation.

Left tackle: As the ball is snapped, charge hard at the outside shoulder of the offensive wingback. Be positive the wingback is not able to block you in. Hit the wingback if he starts downfield. Attempt to slow him up and be sure that, if he gets away from you, he goes to your inside. If you do not make him go to your inside, if he can go by you to your outside, he can block you in. If the wingback moves back on a reverse play, get depth as soon as you charge and become a normal leverage man.

Left guard: As the ball is snapped, drive hard at the inside shoulder of the offensive end. If the end is blocking in on you, flatten your course to the outside so that you cannot be taken in. If the end does not block on you, turn quickly upfield after getting penetration. React normally to the ball.

Right guard: You have a rather long lateral movement. It is necessary for you to charge across the face of the uncovered guard to your left, while being sure that that guard can never block you in. Perhaps a better way of explaining this angle of charge is to state that your right shoulder should contact the offensive guard's right knee. If you are able to make this charge and contact as described, it will be impossible for the guard to take you in. You will also be low and in position to force the play. Having gained this position, react normally to the ball.

Right tackle: Charge past the center in exactly the same manner as was described for the guard. Try to put your right shoulder opposite the center's right knee. Move quickly, and as soon as you have gained the desired point of contact, react to the ball in a normal manner.

Right end: At the snap of the ball, charge hard across the face of your end, closing the inside gap. Having made this charge, react normally to the ball as you would in regular Defense 72.

Left linebacker: As the ball is snapped, take one step to your right, keying your guard normally. If a drop back pass develops, you still will cover your hook zone.

Right linebacker: As the ball is snapped, take two steps to your right before you make any other move. It is necessary for you to get this wide lateral position since your end is working to the inside and the flank is relatively unprotected. As you move to the outside, key your center. Even though your key indicates the play is going to your left, be positive that you do not react back to the left until you are sure the play is not coming to your own outside.

Play of three deep safety men: All three men play regular Defense 72.

DEFENSE 72 RIGHT

This defense is the same as 72 Left, except that the linemen are all charging to the right. Assignments are as follows:

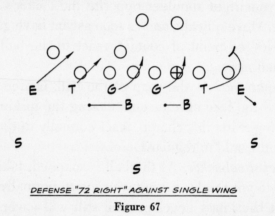

DEFENSE "72 RIGHT" AGAINST SINGLE WING

Figure 67

Left end: Charge flat and fast across the face of the offensive wingback. Be positive the wingback is not able to turn you out. Do not worry about outside leverage on this defense. Force hard to the inside and attempt to drive the blocker back into the play. If the ball goes away from you, get depth and become the leverage man.

Left tackle: As the ball is snapped, charge hard to the inside past the face of the offensive end. Be sure that the end is not able to block you out. Stay flat so that you cannot be trapped out. React to the ball.

Left guard: Charge fast enough to get past the

188

guard to your right. You must never let this guard block you out. As the ball is snapped, make your target the guard's left knee and attempt to contact it with your left shoulder. If you can gain this position, it will be impossible for him to block you out. Having gained your objective, react normally to the ball.

Right guard: Charge the center exactly the same way as you did the guard in Defense 72 Left. Get your head past the center. Be sure that he cannot block you in. Play the ball.

Right tackle: Drive out past the offensive end. Be sure that you charge across his face so that the end never is in position to hook you to the inside. Having made this movement and gained your objective, react normally to the ball. If the ball is going away from you or a drop back pass develops, deepen quickly and force the play. Maintain offside leverage on the ball. If the ball is coming your way, react normally.

Right end: As the ball is snapped, take two steps to the outside and one step back. Play normally from this point.

Left linebacker: At the snap of the ball, take two steps to your left. As you make this movement, watch your guard. Key him properly. Be positive that your first responsibility is *outside* your own left end. Do

189

not be held by any inside fake. Having made your movement to the outside, play your key and react normally to the ball.

Right linebacker: Take one step to your left as you key the center. Play your key, and react normally to the ball.

These two adjustments, played with regular Defense 72, vary the charge of the linemen and should confuse, to a degree, the offensive blocking. By studying the three defenses it is apparent that all linemen from the same position have three basic movements: (1) straight ahead into the opponent opposite them, (2) a radical movement past the opponent to their left, and (3) a radical movement past the opponent to their right. These three variations of charge, since they are vastly different, complicate the efficient execution of blocking assignments on the part of the offensive team.

If the offense, from certain lateral field positions, has a tendency to run to the wide field, 72 Left or 72 Right is an excellent adjustment. For example: if, with the ball on the right defensive hashmark, and wide field to the defensive left, a single-wing team, eighty or ninety per cent of the time, will run a play to the wide field, 72 Left will stop this play effectively. In a like manner, if the ball is on the defensive left hashmark, with wide field to the defensive right, 72 Right becomes a fine adjustment against a team which has a tendency, the majority of the time, to run the ball to the wide field.

Neither of these adjustments is as sound as regular Defense 72 if the slant is called to the wrong side and the ball moves in the opposite direction. However, there is always a chance, if this happens, that one of the slanting linemen will penetrate deeply enough to get to the ball carrier behind the line of scrimmage, due to an offensive blocking error, and stop the play for a loss even though his stunt was to the wrong side.

Other effective stunts against single-wing are to shoot the linebacker through the gap in front of him, or to cross charge the linebacker with the defensive linemen in his immediate area. These stunts were explained in detail for Defense 72 against the "T" formation. They can be used effectively against single-wing although there is always the danger that the double team blocks of the single-wing offense will pick up the shooting lineman almost by accident if the play happens to be called in the area where the linebacker is shooting. But a shooting linebacker who happens to be going through the area occupied by an offensive man who pulls out to lead the play may be able to get to the ball carrier in the backfield and throw him for a loss.

DEFENSE 60 VS. SINGLE-WING

It is always well to have defensive alignments which change the spacing for the offensive blockers. Therefore, in preparing for a single-wing opponent,

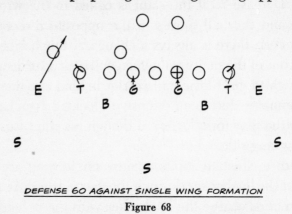

DEFENSE 60 AGAINST SINGLE WING FORMATION

Figure 68

Defense 60 should be used with Defense 72. In playing this defense there is no variation of assignments in adjusting from the "T" to the single-wing. The alignment is exactly the same as against the "T" formation. In comparing Defense 72 with Defense 60, you will note that the defensive linemen are now playing against a different opponent of the offensive team. Assignments for Defense 60 against single-wing are as follows:

Left end: Line up 2 feet outside the offensive wingback. Play the same assignment as was described for Defense 72 against single-wing.

192

Left tackle: Line up shading the outside of the offensive end. As the ball is snapped, charge hard straight into the end, contacting his outside shoulder. Be positive that the end cannot block you in alone. If the wingback drives in on you, fight the pressure. It is a difficult thing for you to hit the end and still avoid being blocked in by the wingback. However, if you are always conscious of the possibility of this block you should be able to fight the pressure quickly enough to avoid being driven back. In driving at the offensive end you should also, by using your peripheral vision, be conscious of the tackle to your inside. If he turns out at you, turn in and fight his pressure exactly as you would in any normal defensive situation.

Left guard: Line up opposite the right offensive guard. React to the three linemen in your area exactly as you would in a "3-on-1" situation.

Right guard: Line up head up with the offensive center. React to the three men in your area as you would in a normal "3-on-1" situation.

Right tackle: Line up on the inside shoulder of the offensive end. As the ball is snapped, charge hard at the outside shoulder of the end. Contact the end. Do not let him cross the line of scrimmage. Hold him up as long as possible. Be positive that he never blocks you in. When he gets away from you, react normally on your regular angle of pursuit. If the ball is going away from you and the end also has moved downfield, get your depth quickly and be the leverage man. You also must get depth against drop back passes as you have outside leverage responsibility.

Right end: Line up 2½ to 3 feet outside of your tackle. React exactly as you would in Defense 60 against the "T" formation. Play the ball with your normal reaction rule, "Ball come, I come; ball go, I go." On drop back passes you should fall off quickly to cover the flat to your side.

Linebackers: Line up head up with offensive tackles 2½ yards deep. (Remember, against single-wing you must be deeper than you are against the "T" formation.) React to the block of your tackle exactly as you do against the "T" formation. There is one exception. If your tackle blocks to the outside as you start to fill, be conscious of the offensive linemen on either side of him. If they are pulling away from the angle of his block, do not continue to shoot the gap but move with the flow of the pulling linemen. If your tackle blocks to the inside, even though adjacent linemen are pulling and moving to the outside, it is safe for you to continue to shoot. You probably will be able to get through the gap cleanly and get to the ball carrier in the backfield.

All other reactions are normal. Play as described for the other defenses.

Safeties: Line up and play exactly as described for Defense 72 against the single-wing.

This defense can be adjusted to 60 Left and 60 Right in exactly the same manner as Defense 72 was adjusted to 72 Left and 72 Right. In each instance the lineman on defense must remember to drive his head outside of the lineman past whom he is slanting. This defense is better than Defense 72 from the standpoint of Slant Left and Slant Right, since it is slightly better balanced and the linebackers have a much simpler job in adjusting and keying their tackles as they slant than they do from Defense 72. Briefly, the assignments are as follows:

DEFENSE 60 LEFT

Left end: Take one step to the outside. Make no move to cross the line of scrimmage. React normally as a defensive end.

Left tackle: Charge fast to the outside getting past the head of the offensive wingback. Hit and hold up the wingback playing exactly as described for Defense 72 Left.

Left guard: Charge past the head of the offensive tackle, contacting his right knee with your right shoulder. React to the ball.

195

Right guard: Charge past the knee of the offensive guard contacting his right knee with your right shoulder. React to the ball.

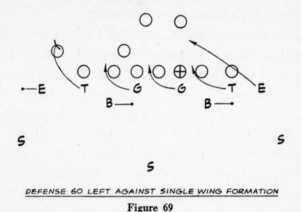

DEFENSE 60 LEFT AGAINST SINGLE WING FORMATION

Figure 69

Right tackle: Slant fast to the inside contacting the offensive tackle's right knee with your right shoulder. React to the ball.

Right end: Slant fast and hard to the inside. Your course should be across the hip of the offensive end at a spot between the offensive fullback and blocking back. Continue on this course. Close the inside gap even though the ball is coming at you. Continue to penetrate until the ball is at least as wide as you are, at which time you may stop penetrating and try to adjust back to the outside. Never anticipate that the ball will go outside of you. If you stop penetrating and work to the outside too soon you will open up a tremendous gap between yourself and the tackle. If, when you make this charge, the ball is moving away from you or a drop back pass develops, deepen quickly and keep leverage.

Fullback and center: Take one step to the right. React to the movement of your tackle as you make this move. Play your key and the ball normally.

DEFENSE 60 RIGHT

Left end: Play exactly as described for Defense 72 Right.

Left tackle: Charge hard to the inside. Contact the tackle's left knee with your left shoulder. React to the ball.

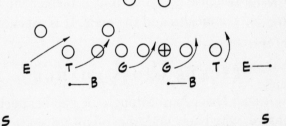

DEFENSE 60 RIGHT AGAINST SINGLE WING FORMATION

Figure 70

Left guard: Charge hard to your right. Contact the left knee of the guard with your left shoulder. Play the ball.

197

Right tackle: Charge to the outside shoulder of the offensive end. Be sure that the end does not block you in. Get penetration more quickly than you would on regular Defense 60.

Right end: Take two steps outside along the line of scrimmage. Do not penetrate. React normally as an end.

Linebackers: Take one step to your left as you react to the movement of the offensive tackle.

These two defensive variations together with regular Defense 60 complicate the problem of the offense because all linemen charge in three different directions from the same defensive alignment.

There is another stunt which is usually quite effective from Defense 60. This stunt is merely the cross charge of the tackles and the ends. It is executed as follows:

TACKLE CROSS CHARGE

Left end: Drive hard through the gap between the offensive wingback and the offensive end. Drive through the end's hips flat enough to maintain inside position on the offensive blocking back. As you charge on this radically flat course, be sure that you cannot be blocked out. Play the ball. If the ball is going away from you or a drop back pass develops, deepen your course and become the leverage man.

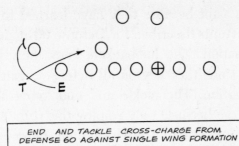

END AND TACKLE CROSS-CHARGE FROM
DEFENSE 60 AGAINST SINGLE WING FORMATION

Figure 71

Left tackle: Line up normally. As the ball is snapped, take one step to the outside. As the end crosses in front of you, loop around him and maintain your outside position on the ball. React normally.

In making this stunt it is sometimes easier to let the end and tackle change positions prior to the snap of the ball. When this is done, both men execute an assignment they already know after completing the stunt. This is, of course, a tip-off to the offensive team if they recognize the change of personnel, but since the defense will be varied in alignments from down to down, the tip may not be apparent.

SUMMARY

In analyzing Defense 72 and Defense 60 against single-wing, it should be apparent that all of the same principles and defensive fundamentals are utilized as were employed by these defenses against the "T" formation. The linemen already know how to make the slant because they have learned to do so from the stunts described for Defense 60 against the "T" formation. The linebackers know how to key properly since they key on all defenses against the "T" formation. The tackle and end know how to cross charge because they employ this stunt against the "T" formation. Therefore both defenses can be adjusted and learned quickly to meet a single-wing attack. It is not a matter of learning a new defense alignment. Rather, it is a question of adjusting defenses which are already well-known by the defensive unit.

A further analysis shows that within these two alignments exist almost all of the possibilities available to a defensive team against single-wing. These possibilities, briefly, are: (1) Line up with different spacing along the offensive front. Defense 72 has normal "odd" spacing while Defense 60 has "even" spacing. Against the interior linemen of the offensive team it is possible to be lined up against any individual on the offense, and by using these two defenses, all offensive men will be covered or uncovered against one defense or the other. (2) From each defense the linemen have three different charges—straight ahead, slant left, and slant right. Since the two defenses vary the spacing, each offensive lineman must learn to play with a lineman on him who charges in three directions; and with no lineman on him, but men slanting at him from both sides. These variations include almost all of the possible complications that an offensive lineman can face.

Because of the simplicity of adjusting Defense 72 and Defense 60 from the "T" formation, and because both defenses, when played as described above, exhaust almost all of the defensive possibilities, they can stop a single-wing attack reasonably well if the defensive personnel is comparable physically to the offense. If the defenses are played soundly against a "T" formation, they are adjustable within a short space of time to become adequate defenses against a single-wing attack.

17

Spread Defense

The majority of modern football teams use the "T" formation. A few operate from the single-wing formation. Occasionally, teams will play the Spread formation.

It is difficult to define a "Spread" adequately. However, for our purposes, a "Spread" will mean any formation that does not have the center-quarterback combination, existing in the "T" formation, nor an intact backfield and line as does the single-wing. If we accept this definition, there is only one other qualifying factor which we must recognize. In the case of a single-wing with one back or end flankered, we would still assume it to be a single-wing formation with a flanker. However, if a single-wing detaches more than one man as a flanker, it would become a Spread formation.

There are an infinite variety of Spreads; therefore the Spread defense must be quickly adjustable and adaptable to any type of alignment, no matter how radical it may be. For example: if the ball is on the hashmark, the center may line up over the ball while the other six linemen take their positions on the opposite hashmark. The backs spread out across the field 10 yards behind the ball. This Spread, although it does not seem sound, could be effective if the defense did not adjust to a sound pattern on the field against this most unusual alignment. The purpose of a Spread defense is to be able to line up quickly and accurately in a reasonably sound defensive alignment against any type of offensive pattern (other than the standard "T" formation with flankers or single-wing with a single flanker).

To understand this defense, it would be best for the reader to review Defense 53 against the "T" formation. (See Chapter 13.) The Spread defense is an adaption of Defense 53. There are a few very simple rules of adjustment, which when learned will insure the fact that this defense will convert to a sound pattern against any type of Spread formation. All men on the defensive team must remember that they are playing a form of Defense 53.

Let us look first at the diagram of Defense 53 against a normal "T" formation. Keeping this alignment in mind, follow these rules of adjustment for the Spread defense.

Right guard: Against the normal "T" you are lined

up against the center. He is the middle man of the offensive line. There are seven men on the line of scrimmage (the rules state *at least* seven must be on

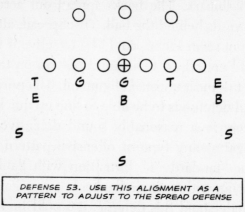

DEFENSE 53. USE THIS ALIGNMENT AS A
PATTERN TO ADJUST TO THE SPREAD DEFENSE

Figure 72

the line of scrimmage). Against any kind of Spread your assignment is to *line up on the middle man* of the offensive line. Do not worry about the position of the offensive center. Pick out the middle man of the seven, and line up on him. (If there are more than seven men on the line of scrimmage, which is unlikely, play on either of the two middle men.) From this position, charge normally against the man in front of you and react to the ball with your normal angle of pursuit. If there are offensive linemen within blocking distance of you, key them exactly as you would on a "3-on-1" drill as you make your charge.

Right tackle and left guard: Take your position in relation to your own right guard. He will be playing on one man. Skip the next offensive lineman between you and him, and line up on the next man. Take your position immediately outside of this lineman. Charge and play normally.

If there is a 5- to 6-yard gap between your right guard and the next offensive lineman, line up just inside your opponent. In this instance, be positive that you can get across the gap quickly enough to keep leverage on the ball. If there is any doubt in your mind as to your ability to do this, use your normal rule.

Left tackle and right end: Look to the inside and take your position in relation to your adjacent teammate. Line up head up with, or shading the outside, of the first offensive lineman outside of your teammate. Charge hard into this man. Hit him, attempt to hold him up. As soon as he gets away from you, continue across the line of scrimmage and become a normal leverage man.

Wide safeties: Line up 8 yards deep directly opposite the widest eligible pass receiver. As the ball is snapped, react normally, being sure that you do not come up unless you are positive it is a running play.

Outside linebackers (left end and right linebacker): Line up directly opposite the second eligible

205

receiver from the outside. (The wide safety on your side will line up opposite the widest eligible receiver on your side.) Your alignment is head up with the first eligible receiver inside of this man. Play about 4 yards behind the line of scrimmage. As the ball is snapped, drop back to a depth of 6 to 9 yards, playing pass first but being in position to come up quickly to support against a running play.

Middle linebacker: Line up directly opposite the third eligible pass receiver. (This position will put you out to one side or the other if the third eligible receiver is a flanker on one side or the other. If the third eligible receiver is in the middle you will be in the middle of the formation.) Because of rule limitations, there can be no more than two eligible receivers on either side, with a third receiver on one side of the other. The rules state that seven men must be on the line of scrimmage. One back must remain in position to throw the forward pass. With the widest and the next widest eligible receiver covered on either side, there remains only one more eligible receiver to be accounted for. The middle linebacker will line up opposite this man. Having done so, the middle linebacker should react normally to the ball.

Middle safety: You are absolutely free in your alignment and should remember that you are "truly" the safety man in this defense. It is up to you to be deep enough to prevent a touchdown on any type of play. Take your position in relation to the middle of the formation and the middle of the field. React and play the ball.

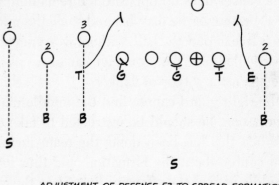

ADJUSTMENT OF DEFENSE 53 TO SPREAD FORMATION

Figure 73

The only difficulty in adjusting this defense to any type of Spread is for the right or middle guard to line up accurately. If he can find the middle man in the offensive line, the rest of the pattern will cover the field quickly and adequately. Even though the guard may be slightly out of position if the offensive line is truly radically dispersed, no easy touchdown should develop since the pattern for pass coverage is easily recognizable by all men responsible for covering the passes. Pass defenders can take an accurate position even though the spacing of the offensive line may be difficult for the linemen. The two wide safe-

207

ties should always be able to find the widest eligible receiver on their side. The two outside linebackers should, with no trouble at all, be able to find the next widest eligible receiver on their side. The middle linebacker lines up opposite the remaining pass receiver, wherever he may be, and since the middle safety is free to play the ball, without worrying about any particular man, pass coverage can always be accurate against any type of flanker.

If the right guard cannot find the middle man in the formation, he should be instructed to take time out. When this has been done, the team members should confer about the formation, and thus locate the middle man of the offensive line. Then the other linemen will be able to take their positions accurately.

To be sure you understand this defense, it would probably be a worth-while drill for you to draw some radical Spread formations. Pay no attention to the spacing that you use, either for the line or the position of the backfield men. Be sure, however, that you have at least seven linemen on the line of scrimmage since the rules of football provide that this must be done. Having diagrammed as radical a formation as you possibly can, use the rules stated above to place the defense. When you do this, you will notice that you have a good pattern on the field against the formation of the offense. Given a good pattern on the field, the containing portion of the defense should be able to prevent the easy touchdown. There are not many forcing men in this alignment, but Spread formations do not need to be forced since the wide areas which exist between backfield men and sometimes even linemen make it difficult for offensive men to coordinate accurately enough to make a steady succession of short gains.

Briefly in review, the rules for the Spread formation are as follows: (1) Right guard lines up opposite the middle lineman. (2) Remaining linemen take their position in relation to the right guard as would be done in a normal five-man line. (Left guard and right tackle: let one offensive lineman take his position between you and the middle guard. Left tackle and right end: line up opposite first offensive lineman outside of your tackle.) (3) Outside safeties line up opposite the widest eligible receiver to your side. (4) Outside linebackers line up opposite the next widest eligible receiver to your side. (5) Middle linebacker lines up opposite the third and only remaining eligible pass receiver. (6) Middle safety lines up in the middle of the field and plays the ball.

18

Pass Defense

In any consideration of defensive football, it is apparent that as the ball is snapped on any down, *the first consideration* is always *pass defense.* The forward pass is the atomic bomb of football offense. Defensively, every man must consider the possibility of a forward pass being thrown on each play. Never for a single play can the possibility of the forward pass be overlooked. Therefore, in any discussion of team defense the first consideration is how to stop the forward pass. Only then can the defense against runs be considered.

This sequence—pass defense, then running defense—must always be maintained. Running defense can never be thought of as a single entity because it evolves after pass defense has been played. At the start of each play the entire unit of defense is playing for a forward pass. If the forward pass does not develop, they then play for the run. They must never play for the run first, and then try to adjust against a pass.

There are two general objectives of pass defense. (1) *Rush the passer* so that he will not have time to throw the ball. (2) *Cover the receivers.* These two objectives are vital to any good pass defense. There is a third general objective which is, perhaps, more important than either of the first two and which is often overlooked by many defensive players.

The third objective of pass defense is to *delay the pass receivers,* and/or, to keep them from running the route or course that they would like to run.

Most forward passes are designed as a well-timed play. On one type of pass pattern a receiver is supposed to go down the field a certain distance, then make a radical break one way or the other, momentarily putting him in the open. The passer, of course, must deliver the ball at the proper time. The second type of forward pass is to run receivers through different defensive zones and thereby spread or deepen the pass defender covering the areas so that an offensive man crossing the field will be open between defensive players.

Both of these approaches to forward pass offense are used by all good offensive teams. If the pass defense is adequately executed and the receivers are delayed and kept from running their proper course, the timing of the pattern itself will be broken down and the pass defense will be far more simple to execute.

The big objectives of pass defense should be not only to *rush the passer* and *to cover the receivers,* but also and, perhaps most important, to *delay the receivers* and *break down the timing* of the pass pattern.

In all of the defenses that have been discussed you will note that a defensive player is assigned to line up opposite the offensive end. Regardless of the alignment taken, this is a sound defensive procedure. If the end is allowed to leave the line of scrimmage untouched, he not only gets downfield quickly, but he also has balance and coordination and can run smoothly, feint cozily, and thereby maneuver himself into an open position to receive a forward pass.

When the end has a defensive man playing over him who charges at him and hits him before he can break down the field, he is severely handicapped as a receiver. In order to catch a pass, he must first get past this defensive player. If the defensive player has good balance and a real determination to control the offensive end, the end will experience considerable difficulty in getting off the line of scrimmage cleanly. It is not possible for one man to hold up an end for a considerable length of time. But even though the defensive player cannot hold him up for long, the fact that the end has been hit, that he is a little off balance as a result of the jolt, not only delays him in starting downfield but starts him off on a course which is not quite as accurate as the one he would like to run.

In addition, the end may be off balance enough to make it difficult for him to catch the quick pass just beyond the line of scrimmage. If the end is free to get off the line cleanly, the "T" formation quarterback can usually throw very quickly and very accurately to him over the line. On the other hand, if the end is hit hard on the line of scrimmage when the ball is snapped, he is not in position to catch the ball quickly because he cannot get downfield fast. He still may be off balance when the ball is thrown.

If the end plays as a flanker, it is more difficult for the defensive pattern to remain sound and still have a man playing opposite the offensive end. But when the end becomes a flanker, the offense loses some of its running effectiveness inside to the side of the flankered end. The offense can still go outside effectively because the end can be a good blocker on wide plays even though flankered. But, as he moves out away from the center of the formation, the strength of his blocking is lost on all inside running plays. One defensive player can usually be detached off the line to play the end "from the inside out," in order to keep the end from crossing the field on a shallow angle. If the end endeavors to come across the field, the defender must make the end go deep behind him. By playing in this manner the detached defensive man also can remain between the passer and the end should he attempt to catch a quick pass 5 to 6 yards downfield. In this instance, the ball necessarily must be thrown over the head of the defensive player. The higher the arc of the ball, the longer the ball is in the air. The longer the ball is in the air, the more time reacting defensive secondary men will have to recover to the ball and get to the spot of the intended completion.

Defensive play against the end is a vital factor in all pass defense. As a general rule, the end should have a man head up with him whenever he is a normal end playing in a compact formation. When the end becomes a flanker, some member of the defensive team should be detached to play him "from the inside out."

This method of play against offensive ends comprises the major portion of objective No. 3 of the pass defense—that of delaying the receivers. The linebackers also enter this phase and their actions in relation to it will be explained in greater detail later.

There are three basic theories of pass defense, all

of which pertain to the pass coverage itself. Regardless of the method being used, all theories of coverage have the common objectives of rushing the passer as hard as possible, delaying the receivers, and covering the receivers. The three basic theories of pass defense are: first—"man-for-man" coverage; second—"zone" pass defense; and third—a combination "zone" and "man-for-man" pass defense. Let us consider, briefly, each of these three methods.

"Man-for-man" pass defense has one obvious advantage. When a defensive player is lined up opposite an offensive player and told to cover him wherever he goes, the defender should never allow the offensive player to get completely away from him. Since his assignment on pass defense is to cover that one man regardless of what his movement might be, the offensive player stands very little chance of completely fooling the defensive player or of getting into the open unexpectedly. However, as against this obvious simplicity of assignment there are two drawbacks which make this virtually an impossible theory to apply in actual play.

In the first place, the movement of the offensive player on a running play may be such that the defensive player who has to play pass all of the time is unable to support the run quickly enough to help the running defense at all, even though the pass receiver that he is trying to cover makes no important block on the play. If the defensive man guesses when the offensive man starts to block, he obviously can be fooled into coming up too soon and thereby letting the man he is supposed to cover get in the clear behind him.

The second weakness of the "man-for-man" pass defense is even more glaring and makes the defense even harder to play.

A football field is a wide open area. If one man must cover one man throughout this wide area, it is very simple for the offensive team to detach one man far to one side of the field and put all other eligible receivers on the other side of the field. This one man now must keep the pass receiver from getting behind him for a touchdown and still must be able to cover him if he starts down the field and hooks or breaks to either side. Very few defensive players possess the ability to cover one man over so wide an area and in all directions. They need support from other members of the defensive team if the pass receiver breaks on a radically sharp pattern, or if he hooks. This is the major weakness of the "man-for-man" type of pass defense.

The "zone" pass defense, if played as a "pure" zone, is very sound against all deep, long passes since the secondary men will be quickly dropping deep and will be attempting to cover the field from side line to side line with a pattern of three or four defensive players. When three or four men play deep in a pattern as a team, they are able to cover all types of long passes.

The weakness of the "zone" defense, however, is the difficulty in covering flat, short, and hook passes. If a number of defensive players are dropping quickly to cover the deep outside and deep middle zones, and if other men are rushing the passer, there are not enough defensive players remaining to cover all of the hook and all of the flat pass areas all of the time. However, the "zone" defense, while weak against this type of short passing, is strong against long passing.

The combination "zone" and "man-for-man" pass defense, in theory, is perhaps the soundest of the three. The idea, briefly, can be stated in this manner. The defense deploys on the field to meet the offensive formation. Men in the defense secondary are assigned to cover various areas on the field. If and when a pass receiver comes into their zone, they cover him in their zone. As he passes out of their zone, they let him go to the next defender. This theory sounds extremely good, and can be played quite effectively. It has one rather apparent, and sometimes fatal, weakness. By running receivers through the zones of different defensive players, defensive men can be carried to the extremes of their zones on opposite sides, and a large opening will result between the two defenders. If a third pass receiver can split this zone, he may be open for a long gain or a touchdown.

For example, the wide safety is assigned to cover the deep outside. If a flanker is placed to his side, and the flanker breaks down the field 12 to 15 yards and then cuts on a sharp angle toward the side line, the wide safety playing a combination "zone" and "man-for-man" will cover the flanker all the way through his zone and will be moved very close to the side lines as he covers the flanker. Meanwhile, the offensive end will drive through the middle safety. As he gets into the deep middle zone he will break away from the flanker, carrying the safety man away from the outside safety on that side. Since the safety man must cover any pass receiver through the deep middle zone, this course by the receiver will pull him through the middle zone away from the flanking man. The middle safety and the outside safety will become separated by approximately 35 to 40 yards. As these two men are playing their zones as described, the opposite end delays slightly as the play starts and then breaks across the field between the deep middle and the deep outside zone. If the mid-

dle safety and the outside safety on that side are
doing a good job of covering the men who first enter
their zones, as described above, the crossing end

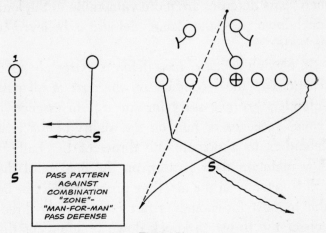

PASS PATTERN
AGAINST
COMBINATION
"ZONE"-
"MAN-FOR-MAN"
PASS DEFENSE

Figure 74

will undoubtedly be open. This type of weakness
is the basic problem of the combination "zone" and
"man-for-man" pass defense.

When the pattern described above is run accurately and the defense plays as described, a touchdown may result. Therefore, it is the opinion of the
authors that a "pure zone" pass defense is superior to
the combination "zone" and "man-for-man." This is
true because of the vulnerability to the possible long
touchdown pass of the combination "zone" and "man-
for-man." As was stated at the outset of the book, the

219

main objective of the defense is to prevent the single play, long, easy touchdown. Since both the "man-for-man" and the combination "zone" and "man-for-man" pass defenses are more vulnerable to the long touchdown pass, the "zone" defense is believed to be better.

In playing a "zone" pass defense, extremely good reactions in the secondary on the part of all pass defenders are necessary for success. In essence, a "zone" succeeds or fails on the ability of the pass defenders to anticipate the throw of the ball. If they maintain their pattern on the field until the ball is actually in the air, they probably will not be able to move far enough or fast enough in the direction of the throw to knock down or intercept the ball. On the other hand, if they can *anticipate* the throw and are moving in the proper direction as the ball leaves the passer's hands, they probably will be able to get to the ball on any pass thrown more than 10 or 12 yards down the field. This instantaneous reaction is the fundamental skill required for good "zone" pass defense.

The proper reaction to the throw of the ball can be developed if sound teaching techniques are used and if the pass defenders remember at all times to *watch the passer* intently as soon as they are sure the play is a forward pass. By watching the passer intently we mean that they actually study his face and his eyes as they move in their patterns on the field. Very few passers honestly fake throwing the ball with any degree of assurance. They may move the ball with short jerky motions, but most passers as they get ready to throw the ball actually "set" themselves and start the throwing motion almost like a pitcher in baseball with a man on base. As this motion starts, all pass defenders must change direction and move toward the indicated spot of the throw. Later in the chapter we will discuss drills which can be used to build up this reaction.

Once this reaction has been learned, the "zone" pass defense will be effective. As has been stated, if the defensive players can be taught to maintain a good pattern on the field they should cover all deep passes and allow no long touchdown passes. By building up their reactions to the throw of the ball they will be able to start in the right direction with increased speed. When they are able to do this, they may be able to intercept a reasonable number of short-to-medium length passes not thrown accurately by the passer.

The "zone" pass defense can be riddled by an exceptional forward passer. However, there are very few exceptional passers in high school or college football. The average college team will face an exceptional passer perhaps once in three or four years even though they may play against a good passer every Saturday in the season. On the average, a good passer will not be able to deliver the ball perfectly more than five out of six times. He may complete five, six, or seven short passes in succession, but when he makes one bad throw and the defense reacts well, an interception will result. Interceptions, as has been stated previously, are a tremendous advantage to the defense and statistics indicate that on the average good passers will throw the interception once out of every nine throws.

It is important that all members of the pass defense realize this fact and *believe it*. The percentage stated above will always work out in the course of a season even though a passer may complete fifteen or sixteen in succession before the percentages begin to work. If he does complete the first fifteen or sixteen, perhaps three of the next five will be intercepted. On the other hand one or two passes may be intercepted in the first three or four thrown. In such an instance the team, and particularly the pass defenders, must realize that the passer probably will complete several before they make other interceptions.

A realization of these statistics helps the pass defense by giving them confidence. The worst thing that can happen for any pass defender or the whole pass defense is to lose confidence. The minute they worry and doubt their ability to defend adequately against a forward pass, they develop tensions which create a tendency to "freeze." If they tense up and "freeze," they will be unable to cover the field. If they cannot react fast—and they cannot when they are tense—they will lose the split second timing in moving with the ball which is so necessary to well-played defense.

Let us now consider the function of linemen in rushing the passer.

Linemen keying properly on the offensive linemen in their area should be able to recognize a drop back pass from the lack of aggressiveness and follow-through in the blocking attempts made on them by the offensive men. Most pass protection blockers will drop back rather than fire out. Those few who do drive out at the defensive team get contact and then begin to protect the area from which the pass will be thrown. They do not attempt to block their opponent to one side or the other. This movement is very unlike the one used when the ball is to be run instead of thrown.

On the running passes, the initial block may be almost the same as would be used on a wide running play. The defensive lineman, reacting normally and moving on his angle of pursuit, will soon recognize the pass because no lineman will be coming downfield.

In either type of pass play, as soon as the defensive lineman realizes that a pass is being thrown, he should use all possible evasive maneuvers in driving through to the passer. He should stay low but should not hesitate to dodge and to change his direction by zigging and zagging as he moves past the blockers.

When he approaches the passer, one of two actions will occur on the part of the passer. 1) If the passer is throwing to the lineman's side of the field, then the rushing man will be confronting the passer. As the passer gets ready to throw the ball, the rushing lineman should raise up so that the passer will have a hard time seeing the field and finding his target. 2) If the passer is turned away from the side of the rushing lineman, there is no reason to raise up. The lineman should stay in the best possible position to continue to rush, to penetrate, and to hit the passer before he throws.

Most linemen make a great attempt to rush the passer, but if the ball is thrown before they reach him, they fail to follow through and complete the play. *It is of paramount importance that all rushing linemen turn and follow the flight of the ball as soon as it is thrown.* If they will do this, moving with all possible speed after the ball, two possibilities remain open to them. First, if the pass is completed (we must assume it is a short pass since the containing portion of the defense will cover all deep passes), the linemen will be in position to recover fast enough to catch the ball carrier from behind should he run with enough elusiveness to avoid the containing backs as they come up to make the tackle. In the second place, if the pass is intercepted, these linemen who drop back and follow the flight of the ball will be in position to block in case of an interception. This vastly increases the possibility that the interception will be returned for a touchdown. Therefore, linemen must not only rush the passer hard, but when the ball is thrown, they *must continue to play the play wholeheartedly* and not become spectators. By turning and going to the ball with all possible speed they may make the tackle that prevents the touchdown or throw the block that allows an interception to go for a touchdown.

There is one other function of the linemen in pass defense. When a passer drops back to throw the ball, the two outside rushers must keep leverage on the passer. If they are careless and get caught inside so that the passer can move out around them, the pattern of the defense collapses completely. When they rush, all other members of the defensive team outside of them will be dropping back. There will be no quick support to their outside if the passer gets around them. They must be extremely careful in rushing not to move in on such a sharp angle that one of the pass protection blockers can block them in, thus letting the passer get out around to run with the ball even though a pass was called.

Linebackers are perhaps the most important part of team pass defense. Their ability will make the difference between the weak and ordinary or the good pass defense. In making this statement, it is assumed that the linemen will be able to rush the passer adequately and that the containing men will be able to keep all of the receivers in front and inside of the containing wall. The linebackers are the individuals who are supposed to move between these areas. Their ability and their movement will determine how well the passes hitting in front of the containing wall are covered.

Linebackers get their first key as to pass or run from the movement of an offensive lineman. If the lineman shows pass, they should drop back as quickly as they can while maintaining their balance. As they drop, they must be extremely careful not to let any eligible pass receiver cross the field in front of them. While moving back, their peripheral vision should enable them to see if an end or a back is crossing from their outside in an effort to get to the opposite side of the field. When the linebacker sees this crossing man approaching his area, he must be positive that he makes the offensive man go behind him.

If the end or eligible back tries to cross in front of him, the linebacker should step up and hit him with a hard shoulder and forearm shiver, attempting to knock him down and stop him from crossing the field. If the eligible receiver attempts to cross the field behind him, the linebacker must drop fast, force the issue with the pass receiver, and move to a depth of 8 to 10 yards before he lets the eligible receiver get behind him to cross the field.

The linebackers theoretically set up a wall against crossing pass receivers that extends from the line of scrimmage some 10 yards deep into the secondary. If they can actually drop quickly, maintain their balance and keep eligible receivers from crossing the field within 10 yards of the line of scrimmage, the pass defense will be much more effective. The overloaded zones will all be downfield and the ball will be in the air long enough to give the containing men a greater opportunity to react to the throw and move a longer distance to the ball.

In playing pass receivers, linebackers should clearly understand the rules governing their ability to hit eligible receivers legally. The rules state that as long as a potential blocker is between the ball carrier and a defensive man, the defensive man may use his hands and arms to protect himself against this potential blocker. When a passer is back to throw, there is no assurance that the ball will be thrown—that a forward pass actually is the play. It may develop into a fake pass and run. Until the ball is thrown, an end or back crossing the field is a potential blocker.

The rule is usually interpreted in this manner: If an eligible pass receiver is moving to the outside, a pass defender can hit him once. If he continues to hit him while the receiver is moving away from the ball and is not getting in better position to block, the play against the man will be interpreted as pass interference. An eligible receiver moving to the outside can be bounced only once. As soon as he is outside of the linebacker, the linebacker cannot touch him and must let him move freely.

On the other hand, if the eligible receiver is moving *from the outside in* at the linebacker, he remains a potential blocker all of the time. The linebacker can continue to hit him in order to protect himself from the possible block. Since this is the situation that occurs when eligible receivers attempt to cross the field, it is possible for the linebacker to protect his area legally as described.

As the play shows pass, the linebacker should
drop quickly as was stated above. If no eligible receiver attempts to cross the field, the linebacker
should continue back as fast as possible while watching the *eyes* of the passer carefully. This is of paramount importance as the eyes of the passer will indicate more quickly than any other part of the passer's body in what direction he will throw the ball.
While watching the eyes, the linebacker continues
to get his depth. When he gets his depth, which
should be approximately 10 yards behind the line
of scrimmage, he should cease to move back, assume
what amounts to a basketball defensive stance, and
watch the eyes of the passer. As the passer draws
the ball back and gets ready to throw, the linebacker
should move quickly toward the anticipated spot of
the throw. This reaction, of starting in the proper
direction before the ball is actually thrown, on the
part of the linebacker is the difference between playing passes well and playing them poorly.

There is a very good drill which teaches this reaction. All linebackers should practice it if they expect
to become adequate pass defenders.

A center, a quarterback, and an offensive lineman
line up on offense with the linebacker in his normal
position to key the lineman and to look through him

to the quarterback. Approximately 12 yards down-field two other men are stationed about 6 to 7 yards apart. They are placed in position so that when the linebacker drops back on his proper angle to cover the hook zone, he will set up approximately between the two men. At the snap of the ball, the quarter-

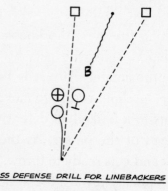

PASS DEFENSE DRILL FOR LINEBACKERS

Figure 75

back drops back to throw and the linebacker drops to cover just as he would in a pass situation. The passer then throws the ball to one of the two receivers, and the linebacker, watching the passer's eyes and throwing motion, moves toward the ball in an attempt to knock it down or make an interception before the ball gets to the target. It is very easy for the linebacker to cover 6 or 7 yards. As he becomes proficient at covering this much ground, the two stationary pass receivers should be gradually widened until they are approximately 12 to 14 yards apart.

If the linebacker drops back accurately when they play at this distance, he will set up in position approximately 6 to 7 yards from each receiver. He should be able to move 6 or 7 yards while the ball is travelling 16 yards in the air, approximately the distance it will have to be thrown if the passer drops back 5 yards from the line of scrimmage and the two receivers are down the field 10 to 12 yards. If each linebacker can actually cover a 12 yard area—6 yards on either side—the two linebackers will be able to cover a 24-yard front, which is half of the lateral field. When they can cover this much distance, they should be able to stop most hook passes.

It is vitally important that the linebackers drop back accurately to the hook zone. This drill will teach them to do so. If a linebacker drops back too far to one side or the other instead of in the middle of the hook area, his distance from one of the receivers will be farther than from the other. The passer, seeing him on this bad angle, should fire the ball to the uncovered receiver. By properly executing this drill the linebacker will soon learn to drop on the proper angle.

As the linebackers become better able to execute

the drill as described, the passer should throw the ball more quickly so that he actually delivers the ball while the linebacker is still in the process of dropping back. This will improve the linebacker's ability to adjust, stay on balance, and move to the ball even though he is moving backwards.

The angles make it just as easy for the pass defender to knock the ball down, even when the ball is thrown at a 5-yard depth. If the linebacker can move 2½ to 3 yards in either direction, he will be able to recover the two receivers, who are approximately 8 to 10 yards apart, 12 yards down the field, since the relationship of the angles remains the same.

The linebackers are, as has been said, the key to successful pass defense. On each pass play they should perform the following steps in order: As soon as they have determined that a pass is being thrown, they should drop back quickly, being careful not to let any eligible receiver cross the field in front of them. They should maintain balance while dropping as quickly as possible to a depth of approximately 10 to 12 yards. As they do these things they must watch the linebacker's eyes and be prepared to move quickly to either side as he starts his throw. If they get back 10 to 12 yards and the ball still has not been thrown they should stop, regain perfect balance, watch the passer, and then move with his throw to the ball.

PLAY OF THE FOUR-SPOKE CONTAINING UNIT ON PASS DEFENSE

The four-spoke containing unit has been described and explained in detail in Chapter 6. At that time the actual movements of this unit on pass defense were not discussed thoroughly. The proper angle of movement and the proper alignment of the men on the field of play in relation to the lateral field position of the ball is the determining factor in their ability to defend against passes.

Since the lateral field position of the ball (its distance between the side lines) determines to a great degree the movement of these men, let us consider them in two units.

First, the corner men: With the ball in the middle of the field, the corner pass defenders will line up approximately 3 yards behind the line of scrimmage and 5 yards outside the offensive end. If a drop back pass develops when the ball is midway between the sidelines, they will drop back and to the outside at an angle of approximately forty degrees from the line of scrimmage.

When the ball is on the left hashmark, the left corner man should line up about 2 yards outside the offensive end and about 5 yards deep. When a drop

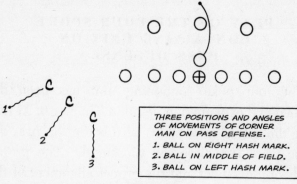

Figure 76

back pass develops from this field position, the left corner man should drop straight back and not give ground to the outside. In the third instance, if the ball is on the hashmark and the wide field is to the side of the corner man, he should line up approximately 2 yards deep and 6 yards outside the offensive end. If a drop back pass develops, the corner man will drop very fast to his outside as he gives ground back. He moves on an angle of approximately thirty degrees from the line of scrimmage.

When the ball is in these three lateral field positions, the corner man will line up in three slightly different spots and will move on different angles: (1) when the ball is on his hashmark and the narrow side of the field is toward him, (2) when the ball is in the middle of the field, and (3) when the ball is on the opposite hashmark and the wide field is his way.

Actually the corner man must learn to move on all of the variations between these three distinct angles as the ball varies from the middle of the field toward the hashmark and from the hashmark toward the wide field. If the corner man can learn to move on the proper angle as the play starts and if he adheres to the following rules, he will maintain good co-ordination with the rest of the containing unit, and the containing unit will cover the field adequately.

The rules of lateral field position for the corner man are as follows:

Until the ball is thrown, the corner man should: (1) *Never get closer than 8 yards from the sideline.* This means that, even though a pass receiver is breaking from the inside out against a corner man, the corner man will let him go to the outside and get between the corner man and the sidelines if the corner man is within 8 yards of the sidelines. He stops moving laterally and moves straight back. While making this movement it is, of course, necessary that he keep the pass receiver in front of him.

(2) If the play is away from the corner man, he must *never cross the middle of the field until the ball is thrown*. This means that, until the ball is in the air and regardless of how the pass receivers move, the corner man will never move further than halfway across the field.

By following these two rules the corner man will maintain his proper spoke-like action in the containing portion of the defense. Of the two, the first is perhaps the more important rule, for if the corner man gets too close to the sidelines, the two deep safeties will have almost the entire field to cover. Two men will find it most difficult to cover the 53-yard width of the football field. Perhaps, in order that there be no possible misunderstanding concerning this rule, it would be best to use the example of a flanker back against the corner man.

If the on halfback comes out as a flanker against the corner man, the corner man's rule of adjustment is to put himself in position to cover the deep outside zone. If the flanker lines up 1 yard away from the side lines, the position of the corner man would be approximately 8 yards deep and 8 yards away from the side lines. Thus the flankered back would be 7 yards outside of the corner man before the play starts.

PLAY OF THE MIDDLE OR DEEP SAFETIES ON THE FOUR-SPOKE PASS DEFENSE

The two middle safeties have the same problems of learning to move at the proper angle as do the corner men. Their movements should be made as follows: (1) If the ball is on the hashmark to the middle safety's side of the field and a drop back pass develops, the safety man should move back and *toward the wide field*. (2) If the ball is in the middle of the field, the middle safety should move back and slightly to his outside at an angle of approximately sixty degrees from the line of scrimmage. (3) If the ball is on the hashmark and wide field is to the side of the safety, he should move *very quickly* back and *into the wide field*. He must get at least 6 to 7 yards lateral movement as he moves the 3 yards back before recovering and getting ready to play the ball. Between these three extremes of movement will be all of the variations of angles as the ball changes lateral position from hashmark to middle of field to the opposite hashmark.

If the two deep men can learn to move accurately on the proper angle, they will co-ordinate with the two corner men and the containing portion of the defense will become a solid wall to encircle at all times all offensive pass receivers. There is one addi-

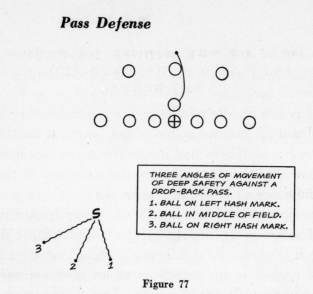

THREE ANGLES OF MOVEMENT
OF DEEP SAFETY AGAINST A
DROP-BACK PASS.
1. BALL ON LEFT HASH MARK.
2. BALL IN MIDDLE OF FIELD.
3. BALL ON RIGHT HASH MARK.

Figure 77

tional rule that the two deep men must adhere to at all times.

As they drop with the snap of the ball on the proper angle to the field they must *never cross the hashmark of the field* until the ball is actually in the air. If they cross the hashmark toward the sidelines, they will be too close to the corner man, and will leave too much of the field unprotected. The remaining deep halfback and the opposite corner man will not be able to cover so much territory. However, if neither halfback crosses the hashmark toward the sidelines, they will always be close enough together to co-ordinate well with each other and, in turn, with the corner men.

All of the angles and plays described above pertain to drop back passes. Running passes present a different and more difficult problem. Against running passes the corner men will react as follows:

When the ball starts toward the corner man and there is a possibility that the play may develop into a pass, the corner man drops laterally and back, maintaining as closely as possible the same relationship with the ball that he had at the time that the ball was snapped. The farther the run continues in a lateral motion the farther outside the corner man will drop. He also will give ground back slightly. When the ball continues to move laterally to the point that the corner man is 8 yards from the side lines, he will stop his lateral movement and will begin to drop straight back. While making this movement the corner man should be alert for support from his safety. The safety will also be moving with the ball laterally and back. As soon as he has progressed far enough in a lateral direction so that he feels that he can definitely cover the deep outside zone, he will call "clear" to the corner man. When the corner man hears this call, he can come up since he no longer needs to worry about a deep pass being thrown over his head.

The most important single factor involved in defending against a running pass is for the corner men (and the other men as well) to *stop their rotation* as soon as the ball stops moving laterally. For example, if the ball starts on a running pass and the leverage lineman succeeds in turning the play in at approximately the original position of the offensive end, the secondary men of the containing unit will have started to move on their normal angles. At the time the ball stops moving toward the sidelines, they should start moving exactly as they would from that field position if a drop back pass were being thrown. Actually, at the point the ball ceases to move laterally it becomes a drop back pass.

When a running pass starts away from the corner man, it is most important that he get his depth quickly, get under control, and watch all eleven men on the offensive team. As long as the possibility of a pass exists, the corner man should continue straight back and keep the entire field and opposing team in view. By moving in this manner he will be able to pick up any delayed receivers moving to his side, and he will also get depth enough to cover the deep outside if the end or halfback from the opposite side crosses the field against the grain of the running fake. It is a fatal mistake for the corner man to angle across the field when a running pass starts away from him. If he does, an opponent can cross deep behind him or a delayed receiver can easily get outside of him.

The two deep safeties react to the running pass in almost the same manner as that described for the corner men. As the ball is snapped, they will move on their normal angle with the ball, giving ground laterally and back. The farther the ball progresses laterally, the faster they will move and the deeper they will angle. They will continue on this course as long as the pass possibility exists. As they make this move they should be conscious of becoming able to cover the deep outside zone. When they feel they are in position to do this, they should call "clear" so that the corner man may move up and cover the flat.

Again it is a vitally important part of the pass defense for the two deep safeties to *stop* their lateral movement as soon as the ball stops moving laterally. If the leverage man succeeds in turning the play in, it becomes a drop back pass. At the instant this happens, the deep defenders should *stop* moving laterally with the ball and revert to their normal pattern of pass defense exactly as they would if the play were a drop back.

It is essential that the four containing men (the two corner men and the two deep halfbacks) maneuver and react as a unit. Because of the way they are lined up on the field of play, they have the offensive team well encircled. If they move together, maintaining the same pattern they had before the ball was snapped, they always will be successful in keeping pass receivers inside and in front of them. If any one member of the unit moves on the wrong angle, the gap between him and his teammates becomes so great that the whole defense cannot function properly. The co-ordination of the four men moving as a team is the key to successful play.

PLAY OF THE FIVE-SPOKE CONTAINING UNIT ON PASS DEFENSE

When the five-spoke containing unit is being used as a defensive alignment, the containing men (ends and three safeties) react exactly as described above in discussing the four-man containing unit pass defense. The two ends and three deep safety men are the containing group. The angles at which they move with the snap of the ball on drop back passes are determined by the lateral field position of the ball.

The ends in this unit operate as follows: (1) If the ball is in the middle of the field, against a drop back pass, the ends will drop on an angle approximately sixty degrees from the line of scrimmage. They should attempt to get about 6 to 7 yards deep and approximately 5 to 6 yards outside of their original position. Having gained this position they should maneuver in the same manner as linebackers. They should assume a balanced position, watch the passer, and move toward the ball with the start of his throw. (2) If the ball is on the hashmark, the end playing the narrow side of the field against a drop back pass should drop almost straight back approximately 6 to 7 yards.

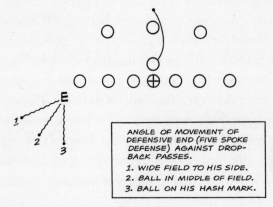

ANGLE OF MOVEMENT OF DEFENSIVE END (FIVE SPOKE DEFENSE) AGAINST DROP-BACK PASSES.
1. WIDE FIELD TO HIS SIDE.
2. BALL IN MIDDLE OF FIELD.
3. BALL ON HIS HASH MARK.

Figure 78

(3) If the ball is on the hashmark, the end defending to the side of the wide field against a drop back pass should drop quickly on a flat angle to a spot approximately 8 yards outside of his original alignment and 5 to 6 yards behind the line of scrimmage.

Between these three basic angles of movement will be all of the other angles which are determined by the varying lateral field position of the ball. If they can learn to move at the proper angles, the ends will maintain a sound pattern on the field, and the seven pass-defenders will adequately cover the entire field.

The end must come across the line of scrimmage against running passes if the play starts toward him. In this situation he is no longer a part of the secondary pass coverage group and becomes the leverage man. However, when a running pass goes away from the defensive end, he should drop straight back fast and then play the same assignment as described for the corner man on a four-spoke defense. The end has the deep outside zone to cover when a running pass starts away from him. He must keep all eleven defensive men inside of him and get deep fast enough to pick up any crossing receiver moving "against the grain" of the run.

PLAY OF THE OUTSIDE
SAFETY MEN

The two wide safety men again have three basic angles at which to move against drop back passes. With the ball on the hashmark, the halfback defending the narrow side of the field will drop almost straight back when a drop back pass develops. If the ball is in the middle of the field, the halfback will drop back and to the outside at an angle of approximately forty-five degrees from the line of scrimmage. If the ball is on the hashmark and the wide

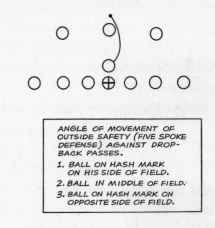

ANGLE OF MOVEMENT OF OUTSIDE SAFETY (FIVE SPOKE DEFENSE) AGAINST DROP-BACK PASSES.
1. BALL ON HASH MARK ON HIS SIDE OF FIELD.
2. BALL IN MIDDLE OF FIELD.
3. BALL ON HASH MARK ON OPPOSITE SIDE OF FIELD.

Figure 79

safety is defending the wide field against a drop back pass, he will quickly drop wide and back on an angle about sixty degrees from the line of scrimmage. The wider the field the more rapidly he must move into the wide field.

All of the variations discussed earlier will be between these three basic angles as the ball's position moves laterally from hashmark to middle of field to hashmark.

245

Pass Defense

On pass defense the outside safeties have two additional rules that they must remember. (1) *Never get closer than 8 yards to the sidelines.* (The reason for this was explained for the corner men who have the same rule for a four-spoke defense.) (2) *Never cross the middle of the field.* This rule is important as it enables the three deep men to co-ordinate with each other and maintain the proper distances between themselves as they adjust to any normal pass pattern.

Against a running pass the wide safety men must first remember that their responsibility is deep and to the outside. If the possibility of the pass exists as the play starts their way, they must continue to drop back and to the outside to get in position to cover the deep outside zone. As they make this movement, they should be ready to move up and cover the flat if and when the middle safety calls "clear." Unless the middle safety is successful in moving fast enough to cover the deep outside, it is the responsibility of the wide safety men to stay back and cover the zone. When the call "clear" is heard, the wide safety will come up and cover the flat area by moving up to the area approximately 8 to 10 yards from the line of scrimmage.

Again, it is vitally important for the wide halfback to stop moving laterally when the ball stops moving laterally. If the leverage men are successful in turning the play in, the ball carrier or passer is stopped in his lateral motion. At that point, the defense reverts to drop back pass defense and does not continue to rotate.

PLAY OF THE MIDDLE SAFETY MAN

The middle safety man has the same problem against drop back passes as do the other men of the containing unit. He must move on the proper angle dependent upon the lateral field position of the ball. If the ball is in the middle of the field and a drop

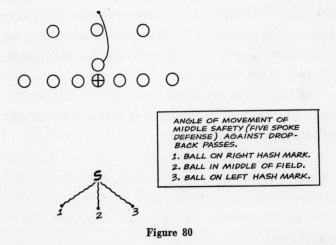

ANGLE OF MOVEMENT OF MIDDLE SAFETY (FIVE SPOKE DEFENSE) AGAINST DROP-BACK PASSES.
1. BALL ON RIGHT HASH MARK.
2. BALL IN MIDDLE OF FIELD.
3. BALL ON LEFT HASH MARK.

Figure 80

back pass develops, the middle safety should drop straight back. If the ball is on either hashmark and a drop back pass develops, the middle safety should drop back and toward the middle of the field. This angle should be approximately forty-five degrees from the line of scrimmage. In between these three angles, again, there are the variations of angles which result from the various lateral positions of the ball on the field of play.

The middle safety should attempt to move very quickly with running plays to either side so that if these plays develop into running passes he can cover the deep outside zone to the side of the running fake. If he is able to move quickly enough to cover the pass receivers in this zone he calls "clear." This signal will release his wide safety up to the flat zone. The middle safety must never call "clear" unless he is sure that he can actually cover the widest eligible receiver to the side of the fake.

The middle safety must also be most conscious of the importance of stopping this rotation when the ball stops moving laterally.

19

Defensive Strategy

The offensive team in football has the initiative. By "the initiative" we mean that the ball is in their control at the time it is snapped. They know exactly *when* the ball will be snapped. By proper execution of the starting count, they should beat the defensive team to the charge. In addition they know *where* the play will be directed, so that from the moment of the snap all of their energies can be devoted to exploiting the weakness in the area toward which the play is directed.

Against these two tremendous advantages the defense has only the limited advantage of the use of their hands and arms. The rules give the offensive team a limitation in that blockers may not use their arms from the elbows down as blocking surface and cannot use their hands at all. The hands must remain in contact with the chest. However, the initiative of knowing *when* the ball will be snapped and *where* the ball is going, far offsets the use of hands and arms granted to the defense.

Because the offensive team has this advantage, the defense must adjust properly to the tactical situation. They must anticipate, as well as possible, the play which is most likely to be run by the offensive team. They also must at all times be very conscious of the effect of different gains against them. All of these elements are involved in what is called the "tactical situation." In order to describe this thought more thoroughly, let us illustrate.

By the "tactical situation" we mean the total consideration on the part of the players on the field of: (1) the down, (2) the yardage, (3) the score, (4) the time remaining in the game, (5) the weather situation, and (6) the field position of the ball.

When a team is leading by one point, the opponent has the ball on their own 20 yard line, and there is only one minute to play a 20- to 30-yard gain without the ball going out of bounds obviously will not do any damage to the defensive team. However, if we change only one of the factors in the tactical situation, everything else is altered. The defensive team is still leading by one point, there is still one minute left in the game, but the ball, instead of being on the opponent's 20 yard line, is on the defensive team's 1 foot line. The changing of this one factor makes a 1 foot gain mean the losing of the contest.

Let us change another factor. The defensive team is leading by one point. This time the ball is on the opponent's 20 yard line. The down and yardage situation is first and ten. However, instead of one minute remaining to play the clock shows 7 minutes left in the third quarter. There is so much time left in the game that sound defensive considerations are more important than any single play. No single play at this point is likely to determine the outcome of the game.

The defensive quarterback must constantly be aware of the tactical situation. In addition, from scouting reports, he should know what plays are favored by the offensive team in certain situations. For example, many teams favor running a particular play eighty per cent of the time on first down. If the opponent favors running off tackle on first down eighty per cent of the time, obviously the defensive quarterback should be in the strongest possible alignment against the off tackle play on every "first and ten" situation.

In a like manner, if the offensive team has a pattern of running the quarterback sneak in their own territory on third down with less than 2 yards to go,

251

the defensive quarterback should be in a defense which he believes will stop the quarterback sneak at the time of this down and yardage situation.

Good teams will not have a truly definite pattern, but some sort of pattern exists for almost every offensive team. The offensive quarterback is prone to repeat plays that have been successful for him in certain down and yardage situations. This is particularly true of *pressure downs.* A pressure down is a play run on fourth down with less than 3 yards to go—downs where a successful play will mean the making of the first down and a continuation of ball control; while, if the play is unsuccessful, the ball will go over to the defense. Scouting reports should endeavor to give this information to the coach who, in turn, should instruct the defensive quarterback to best prepare his team against the play which will most probably be run from a percentage standpoint.

If the offensive team does not have any pattern of particular plays in certain situations, the defensive quarterback should be well aware of the "down and yardage situation" factor of the "tactical situation." Under normal circumstances, a good offensive team will average approximately 4 yards per offensive try. Also, under normal circumstances, super-offensive teams will average about 6 to 7 yards per offensive try. Thus, the actual difference between ordinary and super-effective offenses from the standpoint of average gain per play, is only 2 to 3 yards. The defensive quarterback should keep this in mind. On first and ten the offensive team will probably be able to move the ball for a 3- to 4-yard gain. They probably will continue this advance and make the first down. But, as has been discussed earlier, if the defense can prevent the long gain and the single breakaway touchdown, the offense will be compelled to put the ball in play a great number of times before they reach the opponent's goal line. Somewhere in their march they will probably get a penalty, will fumble, or a lineman will miss his assignment and enable a defensive player to throw the ball carrier for a loss. If any of these things happen, the tactical situation changes tremendously. If on first and ten a normal gain is made, the down and yardage situation becomes second and six. If on the second and six situation the offensive team receives a penalty of 5 yards for off-side, it now becomes second and eleven. In this situation two more 4 yard gains will not result in a first down. The defense can begin to loosen up and play to contain the opponent.

Essentially, the tactical situation hinges somewhere between a team's ability to make the 4 yards and the necessity of making 6 to 7 or more yards to maintain possession of the ball. When the offense is faced with the necessity, to sustain the ball, of averaging 7 yards per try on three successive plays, a sound defense which recognizes this fact will probably keep them from making that much yardage. Three 4-yard gains will pick up 12 yards. Three 6-yard gains will pick up 18 yards. But if the defense realizes that these gains do not hurt them (because of the tactical situation), and they stop the long gainer, the offensive team ultimately will have to kick.

All men on the team should know the situation. But essentially it is the duty of the defensive quarterback to call the proper defensive alignment. The greater the yardage to be gained, the greater the average per try must be and the looser the defense can play.

Linebackers, in particular, must be aware of this fact. Even though the rest of the defensive team is holding to a normal alignment, linebackers should deepen 2 to 3 yards whenever the down and yardage situation makes it necessary for the offensive team to average 6 to 7 yards per try to make the first down. This added depth on the part of the linebackers will make it a little more difficult for them to support quickly on straight ahead plays. However, it is an invaluable aid to them in being in position to cover hook passes, quick passes, and to support wide on running plays. These are the types of plays that are normally used by offensive teams in long yardage situations. Consequently, a defensive linebacker who adjusts properly by deepening his position prior to the snap of the ball on all long yardage situations will in the majority of instances have improved his chances of stopping the play.

In planning for a particular opponent, we believe it is best to play some alignment against which the opponent has not practiced. In earlier chapters we have given a number of defensive alignments in great detail. All of them are sound. At the same time, none of them are particularly new or mystifying to an offensive team. It is a defensive fact that a surprise alignment need not be as sound to be effective as one against which the offense has practiced. If the defense is successful in using some pattern that the offensive team has not practiced against, nor played against, the chances of success from this alignment are far greater than would be the case if the defensive team lined up in a sound defense which can be easily recognized and against which the offensive team has practiced all season. With this thought in mind the coaching problem of defensive football is to adjust the forcing portion of the defense to create blocking problems for the offense.

It is not wise to alter the play of the containing

portion of the defense. If the four-spoke defense is used, seven men remain for the forcing portion of the defense. In a five-spoke containing alignment, six men remain for the forcing portion of the defense. Assuming, for the moment, that the containing men know their assignments and are physically capable of executing them, the remaining forcing men, seven in one case, six in the other, can be deployed and charged in any manner to confuse the offensive team. The alignments taken should be based on scouting reports together with the percentages the offensive team shows in attacking certain areas. Even though the alignment may prove unsound, the gamble will probably be worth the risk if the containing portion plays well enough to stop all gains for 6, 8, or 10 yard advances.

On going in to any game the defensive team should be equipped with four defensive alignments. One defense should be adequate to stop the running attack of the offensive team. The next defense should be able to stop the passing attack of the offensive team either by rushing or by covering. The third defense should be well-balanced against both passing and running in case either of the first two, which are obviously somewhat of a gamble, concerning the play to be run, are not successful. The fourth alignment can best be termed a "victory" defense. By "victory" defense we mean some alignment which is played "soft" in front by the forcing portion of the defense, and which has so many men back off the line in the secondary that it is impossible for the offense to make a long gain or a touchdown. The "victory" defense should be used on all third or fourth down long yardage situations. It should also be used late in the first half or late in the game if the defensive team is ahead and the ball is well out on the field of play.

Within this framework of four defenses, the forcing portion of the defense can be adjusted to give each alignment the strength needed to accomplish its mission. The victory defense should be balanced and can be the same from week to week. However, if possible, the other three alignments should be varied for each game. There are not an unlimited number of possible defensive set-ups, but a coaching staff with ingenuity can make slight variations from week to week, and, if possible, they should endeavor to change their alignment enough as they go from game to game throughout the season so that their opponent can never anticipate accurately what defense will be played against them. The surprise element is the key to successful defense.

20

Conclusion

As was stated at
the outset of the book, defensive football is a difficult problem. Any man can become a reasonably
sound offensive player if he has the will-power and
the desire to condition himself physically and prepare himself mentally. This is true because the
initiative is with the offense. The offensive player
knows *when* the ball will be snapped and *where* it
will be going. He also has been instructed how to
block against every possible defensive variation.
Therefore, by quickly applying rote memory and by
using fundamental skills which can be anticipated
and practiced, the offensive player can play the entire game, in a well-defined, somewhat static situation.

In contrast, the defensive football player *does
not know* when the ball will be snapped nor does he
know where it is going. As the ball is snapped he is
momentarily at a disadvantage since his offensive

opponent, who knows when the ball will be snapped, will beat him to the charge. He must find the ball while ridding himself of potential blockers. He must not be maneuvered out of position by backfield fakes; he then must move to the ball, fighting opposition all of the way, and if he is successful in getting to the ball carrier, make the tackle effectively.

It takes a great deal more athletic ability to play defense effectively than it does to play offense. In a sense, athletic ability is a combination of reaction time, speed of reflexes, and speed of movement. Very little reflex action is involved in football offense. Playing defense is one hundred per cent reflex action to the movement of the offensive team.

In addition to his physical ability, a defensive player must have a fighting heart. As has been stated, he always will be at a momentary disadvantage. If he gives up easily instead of fighting through the initial blocker, he will be unable to play defense effectively.

Since the defense does not know what type of play will be run, it is very necessary that they try to overcome this disadvantage by varying their alignments from down to down in order to create the greatest possible assignment problem for the offensive team. If alignments can be varied without adding any undue mental burden to the defensive team, the total defense will be greatly improved. The offense will have to adjust their assignments and blocks to different men on each play.

In essence, the purpose of this book is to outline simple methods of teaching a squad to play a great variety of defense. To review, a defensive football team is made up of four basic groups of players: (1) linemen, (2) ends, (3) linebackers, and (4) secondary or containing men. Within this framework only the ends need know more than the fundamentals of one group. By employing this system, the individual fundamentals of play for each man are reduced. Defensive players can change their alignment from one position to another without in any way affecting the mechanical method of playing their position.

Regardless of the play of the defensive team, the advantage always rests with the offense since there is no substitute for the initiative which is theirs when they have possession of the ball. The defense must think in the following terms to play effectively:

(1) They hope they can stop the offensive team. (2) They will try to do so. (3) But, more realistically, they will do everything within their power to *delay* the offense. This is a most important mental factor for the defensive team. They must not be mentally geared to stopping their opponents cold—with-

out the slightest gain. If they are, they will lose their confidence quickly if their opponents are able to move the ball well against them. On the other hand, if they expect to see the offense move the ball reasonably well, they will not give up nor will they become discouraged when this occurs. If the offense makes a few gains, the intensity of defensive effort should improve as the players realize that in fighting their delaying action the percentages are beginning to work in their favor.

These percentages will work to the advantage of the defensive team if the defense can always prevent the long, easy touchdown. The defensive team must never allow this fatal error to occur.

If no long breakaway runs or passes occur, and if the defense in fighting the delaying action meets an offensive team capable of playing without error themselves, within a reasonable space of time the offensive team will, by short steady gains, have moved the ball near the defensive team's goal line. Approximately on the 10 yard line a transition in the play of the defensive team occurs. They no longer need to "defend in depth." Instead of having four or five men assigned to the containing portion of the team, in essence all eleven men enter the forcing phase of defensive play. When this occurs the defense must realize that they *can* and *will* stop their opponents short of the touchdown.

By varying the play of the men in the forcing portion of the defense an effort is made to create errors and confusion in the offensive blocking assignments. When this is done, it is likely that defensive mistakes will occur occasionally since football players are not easily adaptable to new alignments and situations, even though their fundamental play remains the same. If the alignment is varied continually, occasional mistakes in the forcing portion of the defense must be expected. For this reason it is best to play the containing portion of the defense in only one manner. If it is played one way, and one way only, without variation at any time, no defensive mistake should ever be made. If no defensive mistakes are made in this area the containing portion will always be able to prevent the long run or the easy touchdown.

In the final analysis, the success or failure of any defense will depend on the desire of the team to become champions. Do they have the innate personal desire to rise above the others to achieve greatness—to develop their abilities to the fullest possible level? If they have this fundamental desire they will be able to carry through a physical conditioning program which will make them as well-conditioned or, perhaps, better conditioned than their opponents. In addition, by doing this, they will develop the physical and mental toughness necessary to be a great football team. This factor of toughness can never be overlooked in any phase of football, particularly defense. If the defensive team is physically tougher than the offensive team they will be able to stop them. This statement in no way implies that the defensive team should play beyond the rules. All teams must play the game according to the rules. However, football is a game of bodily contact. Good, clean, hard-hitting is the essence of the contest itself and, in this respect, a defensive team must be tough if they expect to win. Seldom, if ever, does a football team win if their opponents are physically tougher.

If the defensive team has the desire to win, the physical condition necessary, and plays with greater mental and physical effort than their opponent, they will be able to stop the offense and gain possession of the ball themselves. This objective can be achieved if the defensive players possess these physical fundamentals: First, the ability to react; secondly, the ability to protect themselves from blockers; third, the ability to move quickly and accurately; fourth, the knowledge of the proper angle of pursuit for each man; and finally, the ability to tackle so well that the opposing ball carrier never falls forward.

Conclusion

A team which possesses the mental capabilities stated above together with the fundamental physical abilities stated in the preceding paragraph, can make any defensive alignment successful.

All coaches should realize this point. Football in its final essence is not a game of strategy nearly so much as a game of mental and physical will power, based on a foundation of a few, simple, fundamental physical skills. It is possible to be in a theoretically perfect alignment against every offensive maneuver. Yet, if the defensive team cannot execute their fundamentals properly, and if they have no desire to stop the opponent, the alignment will fail miserably. On the other hand, a defensive team possessing tremendous mental attitude and sound physical skills can line up in almost any defensive set-up and stop a well-conditioned, well-coached, well-drilled offensive team.

Defense is perhaps the primary single factor in winning football. It is virtually impossible for a team's offense to be good enough to cover up for defensive weaknesses. If the defense is not strong enough to get the ball within a reasonable period of time, their offense will not have possession long enough during the game to have a fair opportunity to be as effective as their opponents. Obviously, you cannot use your offense when the opponents have the ball.

Therefore, the first objective in the development of a football team should be the establishment of the best possible defense. If you have a sound defense, the ball will come into your possession many times during the game. If you can couple this defensive ability with sound kicking and sound offense, it is possible to become champions.

Index

A

Adjustments to flankers (*see* Flankers, adjustments to)

Alignments, of defensive units, 54, 85-86, 255-257 (*see also* Five-spoke and Four-spoke defense)

Angle of adjustment, ends, 74

Angle of movement, containing unit pass defense, 233-236

Angle of movement, defensive end against drop-back passes, 242-244

"Angle of pursuit," 55-57, 88

Arm tackles, 25

B

Balance, in linemen stance, 30-31

Ball, lateral field position of, 84

Ball, possession of, 8, 16

Big Seven championship, 5, 10

Blaik, Earl, 55

Block protection, 23-24

Blocking, 2

Bolinger, Bo, 10

C

Center, offensive, in 72 Defense, 95-96

Charges, of defensive lineman, 33-36

"Containing men," in goal line defense, 171

"Containing" of offensive, 14, 16, 17, 21, 52-57 (*see also* Containing unit)

Containing unit:
    adjustment to flankers, 64-66, 69-72, 80-83
    corner men in, 61-66
    deep safeties in, 66-72
    five-spoke, 72-84
    four-spoke, 61, 233-236
    middle safety men, 79-82
    safety men in five-spoke defense, 76-82
    wheel concept, 58-61

Corner men
    adjustment to flankers, 64-66, 236

Index

Corner men (*Cont.*):
 containing portion, 61-66
 co-ordination with safeties,
  237-242
 keying for, 62, 63
 in pass defense, 233-236
 played by end, 91
 in 72 Defense, 97-98
Cross Charge 70 Defense, 156-
 158
Cross Charge 60 Defense, 131-
 134

D

Deep safeties, assignments for,
 66-72
Defense, importance of, 3-6
Defense in depth, 19-21
Defense 45:
 assignments, 114-116
 middle stunt (No. 1), 119-
  120
 middle stunt (No. 2), 120
 middle stunt (No. 3), 120-
  121
 offensive tackle, 116
 right guard, 116-117
 stunts, 117-123
Defense 53:
 adjustment to flankers, 149-
  150
 adjustment to spread formation, 207
 assignments, 137-140, 204-
  207
 charge variation (No. 1),
  141-145
 charge variation (No. 2),
  145-148
 stunts, 141-150

Defense 54:
 assignments, 107-110, 112-
  113
 "red dog" seven-man rush,
  111-112
Defense 60:
 assignments, 124-125, 129,
  192-195
 Cross Charge 60 variation,
  131-134
 left, 195-197
 right, 197-198
 "60 inside" stunt, 126-128
 "60 outside" stunt, 128-129
 stunts, 125-136
 and "T" formation, 199-201
 tackle cross charge, 198-199
 Tight Tackle 60 variation,
  134-136
 vs. single-wing, 192-195, 199
Defense 70:
 alignment, 151-152
 cross-charge, 156-158
 "70 Inside" variation, 153-
  155
 "70 Outside" variation, 155-
  156
 stunts, 153-158
Defense 72:
 against "T" formation, 93
 assignments, 93-98
 left, 102-104, 185-187
 right, 104, 188-191
 stunts, 102-104, 184-191
 vs. single-wing attack, 175-
  184, 185-187, 199-201
Defensive alignments, 255-257
Defensive charge, drills for, 37
Defensive charge, fundamentals, 35
"Defensive keys," 26-28

268

"Defensive stunts," 86-88
Defensive team, basic groups, 260
Defensive vs. offensive play, 258-259
Dodd, Carl, 9
"Double teams," on single-wing blocks, 173
"Down and yardage situation" factor, 252-253
Downs, prevention of, 8
Drills:
  defensive line play, 36-41
  defensive linebackers, 43, 45-46, 229-232
  53 Defense, 208-209
  spread formation, 208
Dummies, for defensive charge drills, 37
Dummies, for defensive linebacker drill, 45-46

E

Eight-man goal line defense, 163, 166-168
Ends, defensive:
  adjustment to flankers, 80-81, 82-83
  angle of adjustment to outside, 74
  as corner men, 91
  defined, 28
  in eight-man goal line defense, 164
  in five-spoke defense, 73-76
  fundamentals for, 47-48
  in running pass defense, 244
Ends, offensive:
  as flanker, 212-214

Ends, offensive (*Cont.*):
  in 45 defense, 115
  in 72 defense, 93-94

F

Five-on-two drills, 39-41, 174
Five-spoke defense:
  adjustment to flankers, 80-83
  alignments, 72-84, 86, 90-92
  containing unit, pass defense, 242-248
  ends, 73-76
  middle safety man, 79-82
  safeties, 244-248
  wide safety men, 76-79
Flankers, adjustment to, 64-66, 80-83, 170-171, 236
  53 Defense, 149-150
  goal line defense, 166-168
  and safeties, 69-72
"Football drive" play, 168
"Forcing" portion, of defense, 52-57, 85-88
Forearm shiver:
  defensive charge, 33-36
  for defensive linebackers, 44-45
  development of, 37-38
  for ends, 48
  for secondary men, 51
Forward passes, stopping of, 210-211
Four-spoke defense, 85, 90-92, 233-236
Four-spoke pass defense, safeties in, 237-242
Fumbles, 8, 9, 15, 25
Fundamentals, football, 2-6

Index

G

Georgia Tech vs. Pittsburgh (1956), 17
Goal line defense:
adjustment to flankers, 166-168, 170-171
eight-man, 163
seven-four, 168-171
theory of, 159
Guards:
in eight-man goal line defense, 163
in "60 Inside"stunt, 127
in "60 Outside" defense, 128

H

Halfback, as flanker, 236
Hand shiver:
defensive charge, 33-36
for defensive linebackers, 44-45
development of, 37-38
for ends, 48
for secondary men, 51
Head, hitting ball with, 25
"Hitting position," 23-24

I

Initiative, of offensive team, 249-250
Interceptions, 222

K

Kentucky vs. Oklahoma (1951), 13, 16-17
Keys, defensive, 26-28

Kezar Stadium (1948) game, 13-14
Kick, blocking of, 9

L

Linebackers:
awareness of tactical situation, 254-255
defined, 28
in eight-man goal line defense, 164
fundamentals for, 42-46
pass defense, 226-232
protection of, 23
reaction drill, 43, 45-46
Linemen:
defined, 28
defensive, in goal line play, 161
in goal line defense, 171
moves of offensive, 43
in pass defense, 223-226
protection of, 23
stance in goal line defense, 162
"uncovered" offensive, 49
"Loose 6" defense (*see* Defense 60)

M

"Man-for-man" pass defense, 215-216
Middle safety man, five-spoke defense, 79-82
Mitchell, Jack, 10
Movement, importance of, 2, 22-23, 27

270

N

National Collegiate Athletic
Association, 89
Nebraska vs. Oklahoma
(1950), 18-19
Neyland, Bob, 8

O

Offensive, containing of, 14
Offensive team, probable errors, 15
Oklahoma, University of:
vs. Kansas (1950), 5
vs. Maryland (1954), 4
vs. Maryland (1956), 9
vs. Missouri (1949), 10
vs. Oklahoma A. & M.
(1952), 10-11
Orange Bowl (1954) game, 4
Orange Bowl (1956) game, 9

P

Parilli, Babe, 13
Pass attacks, and 53 Defense,
147, 207
Pass defense:
against running passes, 239-
242
basic theories, 214-215
combination "zone" and
"man-for-man," 217-219
for corner men, 62-63, 233-
236
drill for linebackers, 229-
232
five-spoke containing unit,
242-248

Pass defense (*Cont.*):
four-spoke containing unit,
233-236
general objectives, 211-212
importance of confidence,
223
linebackers, 226-228, 229-
232
linemen in, 223-226
play of safeties, 244-248
Pass pattern against combination "zone" and "man-for-
man" defense, 218-219
Pass plays, 49-50
Pass receivers, covering of,
211-212
Pass and running defense sequence, 210
Passers, watching of, 220-221,
229
Passes:
drop-back, 244-248
flat, 78
interception of, 8, 15
Penalties, 15
Personnel, categories of, 90
Personnel, utilization of, 89-92
Phases, major, of game, 3
Possession of ball, 8, 16
Practice time, limitations on,
89
Pressure downs, 252
Psychological factors, 1-2, 9
Psychological loss, danger of,
173

Q

Quarterback sneak play, 163,
168, 251-252

Index

R

Receivers, pass, 211-212
Receivers, rules for hitting, 227-228
"Red Dog" charge, 53 Defense, 148
Regular 60 Defense, 129-130
Reynolds, Bob, 18, 19
Rope, use in drilling, 174
Running attacks, Defense "60 Tight" against, 136
Running passes, corner men reactions, 239-242
Running plays, 60 Defense against, 129-130
Running plays, and stunt defense, 123

S

Safeties:
adjustment to flankers, 69-72, 81-82
angle of movement against drop-back passes, 244-248
assignments for, 66-72
five-spoke defense, 76-82
four-spoke pass defense, 237-242
goal line defense, 164-165
movement of, 68-69
Santa Clara vs. Oklahoma (1948), 13-14
Scoring, prevention of, 7-8
Scoring, while on defense, 8-9
Secondary men, 28
Secondary men, fundamentals for, 48-51

Seven-four goal line defense, 168-171
adjustments to flankers, 170-171
assignments for, 168-170
Shoulder tackle, 25
"Shuffle step," of safeties, 68, 69
Single-wing:
Defense 72 against, 175-184, 199-201
Defense 72 left against, 185-187
ends and tackle cross charge against, 198-199
60 Defense against, 192-195, 199-201
vs. defense, 172-201
"Spread," definition, 202
Spread formation:
adjustment of 53 Defense to, 207
drill for, 208-209
rules, 209
Stance:
of defensive ends, 47
of defensive linemen, 29-32
learning to take, 36-37
of linebackers, 42-43, 45
of linemen in goal line defense, 162
of secondary men, 48
Strategy, 249-257
Stunting defenses, weakness of, 122-123
Stunts:
defensive, 86-88
45 Defense, 117-123
53 Defense, 141-150
54 Defense, 111-112

Stunts (*Cont.*):
  60 Defense Cross Charge, 131-134
  "60 Inside," 126-128
  "60 Outside," 128-129
  72 Defense, 99-106, 184-191
Sugar Bowl (1951) game, 16-17; (1956) game, 17

T

"T" formation, defense against, 93, 172-175, 182, 184, 186, 192, 194, 199-203, 213
Tackling, 2, 22, 24-26, 48
"Tactical situation," adjusting to, 250
Three-on-one drill, 38-39, 174
Tight Tackle 60 Defense, 134-136

Time, practice, 89
Touchdowns, prevention of, 12-13, 50, 52-53, 68, 78, 130, 207, 220, 261
Toughness, physical, 263

V

"Victory" defense alignment, 256-257

W

Wide safety men, play of, 76-79, 81-82
"Wide tackle 6" defense (*see* Defense 60)

Z

"Zone" defense, 215-220